A HISTORY
of
BILLINGSGATE

BEFORE WELLFLEET WAS WELLFLEET

by

Durand Echeverria

Maps by Richard F. Lay

Fourth Printing, 2020

THE WELLFLEET HISTORICAL SOCIETY AND MUSEUM

PO Box 58 • Wellfleet MA 02667
www.wellfleethistoricalsociety.org

Cover Design by Robin Parkinson
Book Design by ProCreationsCapeCod.com

CONTENTS

Preface	***1***
Map 1 – The Pilgrims' Voyage of Discovery	2
Introduction	***3***
The Discovery	3
Map 2 – Seventeenth-Century Billingsgate	7
The Geology of Billingsgate Bay	8
The Settlement of Eastham	11
Chapter I The Settlement of Billingsgate	***16***
The Meadow Grants	16
The First Grants of Upland: John Smalley and Job Cole	19
Map 3 – The First Upland Grants	22
Grants of Upland on Bound Brook and Griffith's Islands and near Duck Creek, Silver Spring, and Indian Brook	25
The Agreement of 1694	28
Years of Growth, 1694-1715	31
The Land Divisions of 1711 and 1715	32
The Indian Lands	36
The King's Highway	39
The Land Divisions of 1743	40
Chapter II From Hamlet to Parish	***42***
Squire John Doane	42
The Partition of Eastham	43
The First Ministry of Josiah Oakes	45

CONTENTS

Eastham's Call to Samuel Osborn 46
The Billingsgate Petition of 1718 48
The Billingsgate Conspiracy 50
Hannah Doane and the Deacons of Eastham 53
The Vindication of the Right to Political and Ecclesiastical Autonomy 57

Chapter III The Ordeal of Josiah Oakes ***62***
The Coming of Margaret Hough 62
The Rise of the Anti-Oakes Party 65
The Assessors' List of November 1724 67
The Anti-Oakes Party Takes Control 71
The Second Billingsgate Council, 1726-1727 73
The Ordeal of John Sumner 75
The General Court Vindicates the Inhabitants of Billingsgate 77

Chapter IV Blessings and Afflictions, 1730-1763 ***82***
The Bounty of the Sea 83
The Smallpox Epidemic of 1746-1748 88
The Wasting of the Land 89
The Politics of Growth 100

Notes ***106***

Selected Bibliography ***108***

About the Author ***115***

Maps

Map 1

The Pilgrims' Voyage of Discovery, December 6-8, 1620 2

Map 2

Seventeenth-Century Billingsgate 7

Map 3

The First Upland Grants 22

PREFACE

In 1644 a group of seven Pilgrims sailed from New Plymouth across Cape Cod Bay to begin the settlement of a town they were later to call Eastham. The northern part of the lands that they purchased from the Indians, including a large harbor teeming with finfish and shellfish, they nicknamed Billingsgate after the famous London fish market. Over the years Billingsgate slowly developed from a few scattered dwellings into a community rivaling the parent village of Eastham. In 1723 the Massachusetts General Court gave to Billingsgate political identity as a separate precinct within the town of Eastham; in 1763 the precinct was incorporated as a district with the name of Wellfleet; in 1775 the district was raised to the status of a town.

The following pages offer a brief account of the remarkable history of this colonial village from its origins in the seventeenth century down to 1763, illustrating the grievous difficulties that early New England settlements encountered in coping with not only their physical environments but also the problems of social organization and of political and ecclesiastical governance.

The principal sources of this narrative are the records of the town of Eastham and of its North Precinct, of the Suffolk County Court, and of the General Court of the Province of Massachusetts and the many related documents preserved in the Archives of the Commonwealth.

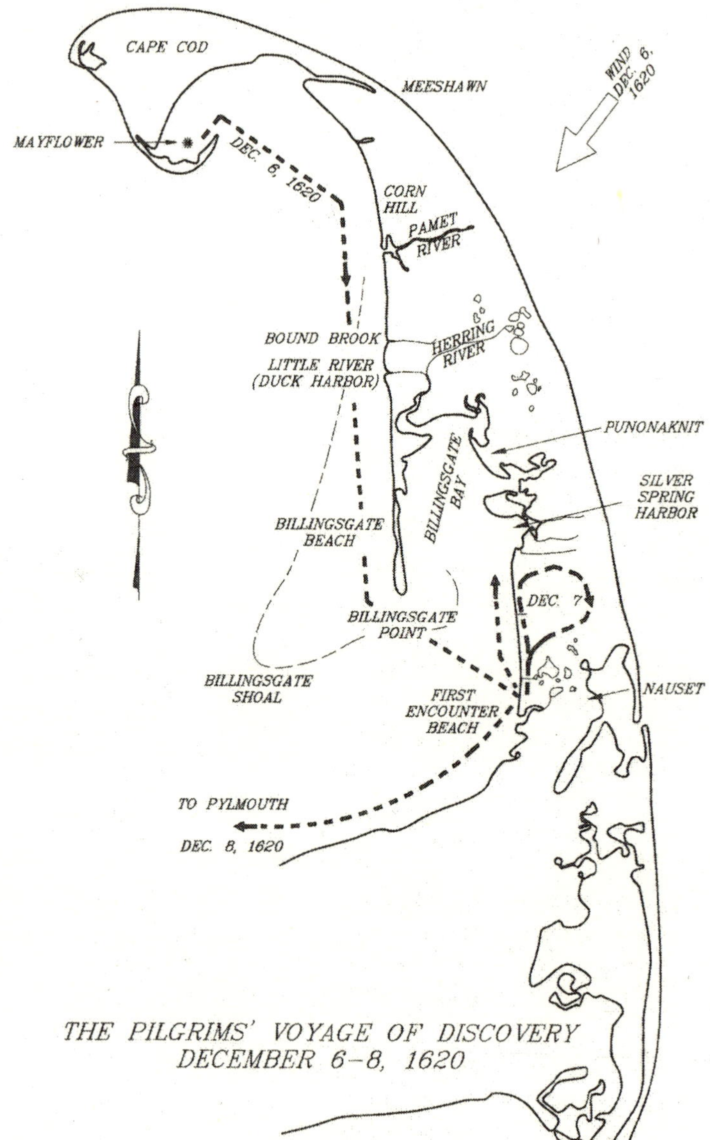

THE PILGRIMS' VOYAGE OF DISCOVERY
DECEMBER 6–8, 1620

MAP 1

DRAWN BY
RICHARD F. LAY

Introduction

THE DISCOVERY

When on the morning of December 6, 1620 a chosen band of Pilgrims shoved off in their shallop from the side of the *Mayflower* anchored in the lee of Cape Cod, the strong northeast wind was so cold that the freezing spray turned their clothes to boards. After weathering with great difficulty the long sandy point enclosing what we now know as Provincetown Harbor, they set forth on their final exploration in search of a place of settlement. Working their way under the lee of the shore to the east, they sailed due south along a wild coast of high banks and dunes. After passing newly christened Corn Hill, where three weeks before they had robbed the Pamet Indians' winter store of corn, and the mouth of the shallow river (the Pamet) that they had fruitlessly explored, they continued on, seeing "neither river nor creek" and failing to notice the mouths of the streams they were later to call Bound Brook and Little River (or Duck Harbor). After sailing on a reach for about six and a half miles along a course parallel to the shore they came to "a tongue of land, flat off from the shore," continuing southward (Billingsgate Beach) and ending in "a sandy point" (Billingsgate Point and later Billingsgate Island). They bore up to round this point, and when they did so they discovered that behind the banks, dunes, and sand spits they had been coasting lay "a fair income or road of a bay" two or three miles wide, extending four or five miles to the north and sheltered on the west, north, and east. This embayment they and their descendants were to call Billingsgate Bay; others in later centuries were to rename it Wellfleet Harbor.

Sailing as close to the wind as they could, they set a southeasterly course toward the mainland. As they drew nearer the shore they espied ten or twelve Indians "very busy about a black thing," which the Pilgrims could not identify. When the Indians saw the shallop "they ran to and fro, as if they had been carrying something away." Continuing their course to the southeast, the Pilgrims at length managed to drag their shallop across the shallow tidal flat north of the (Eastham) Herring River onto what was to be known to history as First Encounter Beach in memory of the attack the Pilgrims sustained there two days later from the Nauset Indians.

The morning after their landing the adventurers divided into two parties, one in the shallop and the other afoot, to explore northward along the shore. Those in the shallop reported that they could find neither river nor creek emptying into the bay, so it appears probable that they did not proceed as far north as Silver Spring Harbor, into which four creeks flow. The group afoot crossed two "becks" of fresh water so narrow that "one might stride over them" (probably Herring Brook and the rivulet at Camp Ground Landing) before coming to the spot on the beach "a league or two" north of their landing place where they had seen the Indians. The mysterious object they had descried from the shallop turned out to be a stranded blackfish (or pilot whale or grampus). The location where the Indians were butchering this small whale must have been well south of the mouth of Indian Brook (Hatches Creek), the present Wellfleet-Eastham boundary. The depiction on the Wellfleet town seal of the Pilgrims landing beside the blackfish and greeting welcoming Indians is of course apocryphal; not one of this band of Pilgrims set foot in Billingsgate (the present Wellfleet) or sailed in Wellfleet Harbor.

After discovering the blackfish the Pilgrims explored some distance inland, finding many indications of habitation but encountering no Indians, and they returned at nightfall to the beach to rejoin the shallop and regain their original landing place. At five o'clock the next morning they were attacked by the Nausets, but neither party suffered any casualty. Judging prudence to be the better part of valor, the Pilgrims hastened to reembark and continue their explorations westward along the shores of Cape Cod Bay until eventually they reached Plymouth Harbor.

The narrator[1] whose account we have been following does not say whether it was this hostility or the disappointing findings of their explorations or their pilot's report of a better site across the bay (at Plymouth) or perhaps even merely the continuing northeast wind that persuaded the Pilgrim explorers to forbear exploration of the embayment to the north whose entrance they had merely traversed and to abandon all thoughts of settling on Cape Cod.

They intended to establish not a trading or a fishing port but a farming village. The excellent anchorage they had found for the *Mayflower* in what was to be Provincetown Harbor had held no attraction when offset by the meager resources ashore. That they, and their descendants, might make a good living from the finfish, shellfish, wildfowl, whales, and seals of the Lower Cape harbors and from the lush bordering salt meadows apparently did not occur to them at this time, or for some time later.

An earlier voyager, Samuel de Champlain, who had explored these same waters fourteen years before, had been more venturesome and had sailed up into Billingsgate Bay and discovered its great oyster beds, which had moved him to christen his newfound haven Port aux Huistres (Oyster Harbor).

Since the Archaic Period of Amerindian prehistory, perhaps as long ago as 2,000 B.C., these great oyster beds and the abundance of other shellfish had helped to sustain an Indian population around the shores of the harbor and along its several estuaries. The Punonakanit village visited by Champlain had developed a stable, sedentary economy based, during the warmer months, on agriculture supplemented by hunting and gathering, and largely on shellfish harvesting during the winter. Instead of migrating seasonally between the seashore and the interior, as did most maritime New England Indians, the Punonakanits, like the neighboring Pamets and Nausets, found all their sustenance within range of the harborside. The large ossuary, a multiple secondary burial, discovered in 1979 on Indian Neck in Wellfleet is convincing evidence of the permanence and economic and social stability of the local prehistoric population.

The Pilgrims' first winter at Plymouth brought suffering and starvation, and until the next summer's crops could be harvested their greatest immediate need was food. In desperation they turned to the lands across the bay from Plymouth, trading with the Nauset Indians for corn but also investigating the fisheries. It did not take the Pilgrims long to explore thoroughly the great embayment they had passed by in December 1620, and like Champlain they were amazed by the size of the oyster beds, the quantities of quahogs, and the numbers of bass, bluefish, herring, and perch that abounded in the harbor and the Herring River flowing into its northwest corner. To their hungry eyes these waters must have appeared a veritable fish market, and inevitably sooner or later some wit nicknamed it Billingsgate after the famous London market, as well known for its oysters as for its foulmouthed fishwives. The name stuck and became the general name for the entire area and the generic adjective for its features. Thus the harbor became Billingsgate Bay, the long sand spit to the west Billingsgate Beach, its tip Billingsgate Point, the shallow waters to the west Billingsgate Shoal, and the salt meadows at the head of the harbor Billingsgate Meadows. Likewise all the area from Bound Brook on the north to Indian Brook on the south was commonly called Billingsgate or Little Billingsgate.

SEVENTEENTH-CENTURY BILLINGSGATE

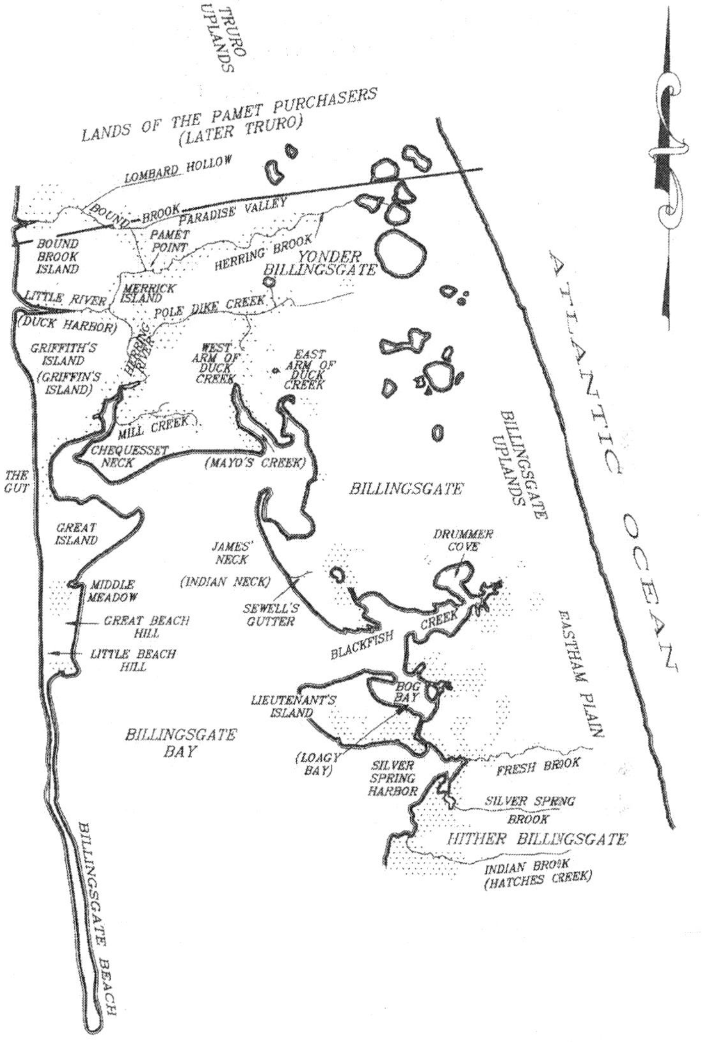

BILLINGSGATE POINT (ISLAND)

MAP 2

DRAWN BY RICHARD F. LAY

THE GEOLOGY OF BILLINGSGATE BAY

Billingsgate Bay was one of the creations of the last of the great glaciers, which dumped on the ancient bedrock of the continental shelf an inchoate mass of sand, gravel, clay, and boulders. For the past 12,000 years the winds, waves, and tides and the rising level of the sea have been refashioning this raw material into its present shapes. It has been supposed that an area of Cretaceous and Tertiary rocks lay along the axis of the present Lower Cape and Stellwagen Bank and that the advancing ice tended to split upon these rocks into two lobes-the Cape Cod Bay Lobe, which advanced across a broad front as far south as Nantucket and Martha's Vineyard, and, to the east, the South Channel Lobe, which filled the thirty-mile-wide channel between Nantucket Shoals and Georges Bank. The dividing ridge between the Cape Cod Bay Lobe and the South Channel Lobe was probably left uncovered until it was overwhelmed from both sides by the two glaciers, which filled the space with sand, gravel, clay, boulders, and masses of buried ice, thus forming the interlobate moraine which was to become the Lower Cape and of which Billingsgate Bay was to be the most prominent feature.

Between the low plains of Eastham and those of North Truro rise the Billingsgate (Wellfleet) and Truro high plains or uplands extending from Blackfish Creek to the escarpment north of the site of Highland Light. This elevated plain is a region of steep hills rising as high as 180 feet, of deep kettle holes, many containing ponds or swamps, formed thousands of years ago by melted masses of buried ice, and of westward sloping valleys, known to geologists as pamets but to the English settlers as hollows, down which once had coursed outwash streams of meltwater.

When the last ice vanished, the interlobate moraine it left behind must have been very different from the land the Pilgrims explored. The heaps of glacial drift had extended far beyond the shorelines of 1620 on both the east and the west, and the two coasts had originally been very irregular. As the sea, replenished by the melted glacial ice, slowly rose, the waves and alongshore currents on the ocean side, acting like a giant shaver, eroded back the indented primeval shoreline a distance of about two miles to the moraine's highest crest, creating the long, gently curving line of high marine scarps stretching from Nauset Marsh to High Head. These forbidding cliffs offered no haven to ships driven by northeast gales upon these deadly strands. As the crew of the *Mayflower* discovered in 1620, the tall scarps were flanked by rocky shoals, vestiges of the eroded moraine. Atop the cliffs the densely wooded hills, dry, wind-wracked, and deserted, long remained useless to both hunter and farmer. But it was in these highlands that the westward sloping hollows found their lifegiving sources.

On the western side of the moraine, from Bound Brook south to the Eastham plain, the advancing and retreating Cape Cod Lobe had left behind ranks of hills or islands of glacial drift separated from each other and from the main body of the moraine by relatively deep and narrow valleys, generally tending to the west, gouged by the outwash streams descending the hollows from the east. As these valleys became flooded by trapped meltwater and the rising sea level, the glacial hills were transformed into true islands or peninsulas, situated originally so as to form a rough tripod with its apex to the north.

The western leg, which had once curved southwesterly from High Head in North Truro out into Cape Cod Bay, had by 1620 been eroded below the surface of the sea, but the ancient shoreline could still be traced by the western edge of Billingsgate Shoal (Map 1). The middle leg was composed of Bound Brook, Griffith's (Griffin), Great, Great Beach Hill, Little Beach Hill, and Billingsgate Islands and had once included an unnamed island that in prehistoric times had existed still farther to the south. As on the ocean shore, waves and alongshore currents had eroded the western edges of these islands of the middle leg and had built up sand spits, known as rombolos, joining Griffith's, Great, Great Beach Hill, Little Beach Hill, and Billingsgate Islands, and by 1620 these currents were also threatening to build bars across the mouths of Bound Brook (north of Bound Brook Island) and of Little River (between Bound Brook and Griffith's Islands). The eastern leg of the tripod was composed of Bound Brook (the apex) and Merrick Islands, Chequesset Neck, Indian Neck, and Lieutenant's Island.

During the final stage of the glaciation a large lake had formed between the middle and eastern legs. On the north it extended to an embayment situated between Pamet Point, Bound Brook Island, and Merrick Island and spread out on both sides of Chequesset Neck, Indian Neck, and Lieutenant's Island. Thence it curved southwesterly and westerly along the shores of the Eastham plain and the Middle and Upper Cape.

After the final retreat of the ice and the merging of this glacial lake with the waters of Cape Cod Bay, the numerous streams and estuaries flowing into the harbor from pamets dredged by outwash streams became, as the sea level rose, submerged valleys subtidal for considerable distances inland. The Herring River system once had perhaps as many as five outlets: the present mouth; Little River (Duck Harbor); an outlet through the present Gut into Cape Cod Bay; Bound Brook, linked to the Herring River by a connecting creek; and perhaps an outlet from Pole Dike Creek out through the West Arm of Duck Creek (Mayo's Creek). This system's tributaries included, besides Herring Brook, Lombard Hollow Brook, Bound Brook (flowing out of springs in Paradise Valley), Pole Dike Creek and its several tributaries, and Mill (Snake) Creek. The other estuaries and tributaries emptying into the harbor included the West and East Arms of Duck Creek, Sewell's Gutter, Middle Meadow, and Blackfish Creek (or River). The latter drew its waters from Drummer Cove, Bog (Loagy) Bay, and the extensive salt marshes east of Indian Neck and Bog Bay. Lastly, south of Lieutenant's Island a bundle of brooks flowed into Silver Spring Harbor: Fresh Brook, Silver Spring Brook, Indian Brook (Hatches Creek), and several rivulets draining marshes on the northern shores of this small embayment.

As the sea level continued to rise, at a rate of about one meter every 1,000 years, the tides penetrated farther inland, creating new marshes. At the same time, however, as we have noted, sand spits were forming between the islands in the axis from Bound Brook Island to Billingsgate

Island-across the mouths of Bound Brook and Little River and across the ancient outlet of the Herring River directly into Cape Cod Bay at the Gut and in the forms of tombolos between Great, Great Beach Hill, Little Beach Hill, and Billingsgate Islands. These gradual closures over the course of thousands of years increasingly restricted tidal flows, particularly in the Herring River estuary (notably in Bound Brook and Little River) but also in the two arms of Duck Creek, thus accelerating the silting of these tributaries. Despite the ever rising sea level, as this process continued the valleys dividing the islands and necks from one another and from the mainland gradually evolved from open water to tidal flats to low marshes to brackish fresh marshes to high marshes, and finally to the shrubby wet meadows we see today.

Throughout this long process, still going on in 1620, these streams and estuaries continued to pour large quantities of fresh water into Billingsgate Bay, lowering the salinity to a level which favored the growth of oysters. Moreover these tributaries also brought from the fresh and salt marshes through which they flowed a rich supply of nutrients, which formed the base of the food chain supporting shellfish, finfish, marine mammals, and sea and shore birds. Lastly, the siltation was creating the wet meadows which were to provide fodder for the horses, cattle, and sheep of the first settlers of Billingsgate.

THE SETTLEMENT OF EASTHAM

By 1643 the Pilgrims had perceived that they had not chosen wisely in establishing the seat of their colony at Plymouth, which was neither a good port nor an area well suited to farming. Newcomers, and some of the original settlers as well, instead of expanding the original village had created outlying towns: Scituate in 1636, Duxbury in 1637, Sandwich, Barnstable, Yarmouth and Taunton in 1639, and Marshfield in 1641. Consequently a plan was conceived to transfer to a better site both the population of Plymouth and the seat of government. In 1644 a committee was appointed to examine lands at Nauset and make purchases from the Indians with a view to reestablishing there the Plymouth church and court. This committee, which included some of the colony's leading citizens, was composed of Edward Bangs, Josiah Cook, John Doane, Richard Higgins, Thomas Prince, John Smalley, and Nicholas Snow. They reported that the area around Nauset was not large enough to support the entire population of Plymouth and furthermore that it lacked a practicable harbor and was too far removed to serve as the colony's capital. Nevertheless they found the land well suited to their own private purposes. So they proceeded to purchase from Mattaquason, the sachem of Manamoyick, lands at Pochet and from George, sachem of the Nausets, land as far north as Indian Brook. Enoch Pratt, the earliest and one of the best of the local historians, told, apparently on the authority of an oral tradition, the story that the purchasers "asked who owned Billingsgate, which was understood to be all the land north of the territory purchased of George the sachem. The Indians said no one owned it. Then, said the purchasers, the land is ours. They answered, it is."[2] Later, the story continues, an Indian known as Lieutenant Anthony, who claimed to be the sachem of the Punonakanits in Billingsgate, sold to the committee all the land from Indian Brook north to a stream known to the Indians as Sapokonisk but renamed by the English Bound Brook, the traditional boundary between the Punonakanits and the Pamets. He reserved for his band's use only a "small neck" called Tuttomnest.[3] This was undoubtedly the peninsula known in the seventeenth and eighteenth centuries as James' Neck and later as Indian Neck, which in 1716 was reserved by vote of the Eastham town meeting for the exclusive use of the Punonakanit or Billingsgate Indians. Lieutenant's Island may well have been named for Lieutenant Anthony, but it does not appear to have been set aside for the benefit of the Indians, for in 1662 the town meeting voted to reserve it for "publick use" and in 1673 ordered that it be used only for the support of the ministry.

In any case, the seven members of the committee, who came to be known as the Purchasers, assumed that by their negotiations with the Indians they had the right to consider themselves the virtual proprietors of Billingsgate as well as of Nauset and Pochet. Consequently at their request the Court at Plymouth issued to them on March 3, 1645 the following grant:

> *The Court doth graunt unto the church of New Plymouth, or those that goe to dwell at Nossett, all that tract of land lying betweene sea and sea, from the Purchasors bounds at Naumskeckett to the Hering Brooke at Billingsgate, with the said Hering Brooke and all the meddowes on both sides the said brooke with the great Basse Pound there, and all the meddowes and islands lying within the said tract.*

The "Purchasers bounds at Naumskeckett" (Namskaket) referred to the 1640 grant of a tract extending "from the [eastern] bounds of Yarmouth, three miles to the eastward of Naumskeckett and from sea to sea crosse the neck of land," made to the so-called "Purchasors" or "Old Comers" of Plymouth Plantations, Governor Bradford and his associates, in compensation for their relinquishment of certain rights.[4]

From the language of the grant of 1645 we may reasonably infer that the name Billingsgate had by that date become common usage and that certain features such as the salt meadows and "the great Basse Pound" (probably the widening of the Herring River at the southeast corner of Griffith's Island) were well known to the Nauset Purchasers and other Pilgrims.

The original seven Purchasers were soon joined by seven more, Daniel Cole, Job Cole, John Freeman, Samuel Hix, John Jenkins, Joseph Rogers, and Robert Wixam. These fourteen men (and later their heirs and assigns) constituted the new body of Purchasers, who as the owners of the lands bought from the Indians and as grantees of the grant of March 1645 were the legal proprietors of all the common and undivided land within the town's boundaries. They also constituted initially the governing body, or meeting, of the town and until 1694 assumed the power to grant – largely but not exclusively to themselves or their heirs or assigns – dwelling lots and parcels of woodland and meadowland. Some of the Purchasers accumulated extensive holdings. Nicholas Snow, one of the original seven, was allotted a total of 170 acres of upland and twenty of meadow in a number of dispersed grants from

Namskaket to Pamet. Newcomers found it more difficult to acquire land, but they did in some cases receive direct grants, and of course they were able to buy land from the Purchasers. Indeed a very active real estate market developed in Eastham during the seventeenth century. Lots of salt meadow were more frequently allotted as original grants to newcomers, and these parcels frequently changed hands.

The political organization of the community was not long delayed. The town of Nauset was incorporated in 1646 and in 1651 its name was changed to Eastham. The meetings of Purchasers evolved into town meetings, which besides making land grants elected officers such as selectmen, constables, and delegates to the Court at Plymouth, appointed committees, enacted regulations, exercised police powers, and taxed, borrowed and appropriated money. Almost immediately the political boundaries of the town began to be extended to the north and south. The northern growth was in part the result of the development of fishing off Cape Cod (now Provincetown). In October 1650 Thomas Prince in association with William Paddy of Duxbury and Miles Standish of Plymouth was granted by the Court at Plymouth a monopoly of the bass fishing off Cape Cod together with the right to use lands, creeks, and timber for this purpose in whatever places he might choose. Furthermore the Court gave to Prince the right "to purchase what lands yet remaineth on that side Cape Cod unpurchased from the true propriators [sic] of them." In 1654 the boundaries of Eastham were extended northward to "Easteren Harbour" (East Harbor) in what is now North Truro, thus encompassing most of the land made available to Prince. Fourteen years later the remaining lands adjacent to the Cape Cod fisheries as well as an extensive area to the south were annexed to Eastham when it was ordered "that Paomet and soe far as the Cape Head [Race Point] be reputed within the constablewicke of Eastham .. . [and] that the lands at Mannamoite [Manamoyick] be att present reputed to be in the constablewicke of Eastham and liable to pay publicke charges there." Then in 1674 "Mannamoiett," "Paornit," and "Satucket" (near Yarmouth) were declared parts of Eastham. This seems to have been the moment of the town's maximum jurisdiction.[5]

Those who purchased lands from the Indians north of Bound Brook organized themselves, apparently on their own initiative, as the Pamet Proprietors. The earliest date in their surviving records is 1694, but Thomas Prince seems to have made purchases from the Indians as early as the 1650s. The Plymouth records show a purchase of a tract by Thomas Paine from Prince in 1670 and another purchase in 1673. There are also references to a division of Pamet lands in 1689. At some time before 1691 a stone monument was erected near the mouth of Bound Brook to mark the southern boundary of the lands of the Pamet Proprietors.

Nevertheless and despite these acknowledgements of the fact that the Plymouth Court's authorizations to the Pamet Proprietors to purchase lands from the Indians had been granted later than and independently of the 1645 grant to the Eastham Purchasers, the Pamet lands from Bound Brook northward to the tip of Cape Cod remained politically part of Eastham until 1705, when they were incorporated as the District of Dangerfield, which in 1709 was made the town of Truro.

In 1656 the Court at Plymouth had enacted a law requiring the towns of the colony to keep records of their divisions and sales of common lands. Consequently in 1658 a committee for this purpose consisting of Josiah Cook, John Freeman, Nicholas Snow, Richard Sparrow, and Robert Wixam was appointed by the Eastham town meeting to bring order out of the mounting confusion in property rights and records. A few land grants had already been recorded in town meeting records as early as 1654, but by reason of the new committee a large number of such entries suddenly appear under the date 1659. Obviously most of these were delayed recordings of grants made at various earlier times.

Chapter I

THE SETTLEMENT OF BILLINGSGATE

The uncertainty surrounding the early grants makes it difficult to determine the first date when land was privately acquired in the Billingsgate area, whether meadowland or upland for a dwelling lot, and there is no record of when the first house was built.

THE MEADOW GRANTS

The seventeenth-century inhabitants of Eastham and Billingsgate practised a hay and forage economy. Hay was gathered from salt meadows extending from Namskaket to Bound Brook-Boat Meadow, Great Meadow, Rock Harbor, Pochet, Silver Spring, Blackflsh Creek, Billingsgate Meadow, Duck Creek, the Herring River, Little River, and Pamet Point. The first house lots, usually of twenty acres of upland, which the town meeting assigned to the Purchasers were along the shores of Nauset Marsh and the Town Cove and in Pochet. Consequently the early meadow grants were mostly in salt meadows at convenient distances at Boat Meadow, Great Meadow, Rock Harbor, Namskaket, Little Skaket, and Pochet. The supply of such easily accessible hayfields was soon exhausted, however, and the town meetings began to grant meadows farther north in Billingsgate at Silver Spring Brook, around the head of Blackfish Creek and along its southern banks (notably at a place the Indians called Peteponnetuksett or Poteponatucket), in Billingsgate Meadow at the head of the harbor between the West Arm of Duck Creek and the Chequesset Neck cliffs, along the Herring River and Little River, in the meadows east and north of Bound Brook Island, and around Coles Neck. Most of these meadow grants, about fifty covering some 75 acres, were made by 1659, and some 35 of these, averaging about one acre each, were located in Billingsgate Meadow. Of the latter group at least nineteen were contiguous and nearly all the other nearby lots were clustered in abutting groups of two to six grants. It is obvious that virtually all the good meadowland had been parceled out before 1660.

These meadows were the principal sources of fodder for horses, cattle, and sheep during the winter months. Since there is no record of the existence of barns in Billingsgate as early as 1659, it may be assumed that the hay was carted to the settled part of Eastham. Evidence indicates that the ancient Indian trail from Nauset to Pamet had by the 1650s been broadened to a rough cart way that ran north from the Eastham meeting house past the appropriately named Halfway Ponds, around the heads of Indian Brook, Fresh Brook, Blackfish Creek, and Duck Creek, across Herring Brook a quarter of a mile west of Herring Pond, and from there around the head of the Pamet River. This road, which was later to become the county road or King's Highway, divided in several branches leading to meadows: one along the southern banks of Blackfish Creek (the present Old Wharf Road, but branching off further south); another from a point north of Duck Creek to Billingsgate Meadow and Chequesset Neck; and a third, known as the Pamet Path, parallel to the Herring River downstream to the meadows east of Bound Brook Island and from there north to the mouth of the Pamet River.

Until the Agreement of 1694 (of which we shall speak presently) no upland of any sort in Billingsgate was granted to anyone except the fourteen Purchasers or their heirs or assigns. There was, however, no obstacle to the granting of meadow lots in Billingsgate to newcomers. This was notably true during the years through 1659, a period during which new settlers in fact received more meadow lots in Billingsgate than did Purchasers or their heirs or assigns.

During the years from 1660 to 1703, however, we see a marked decrease in the number of meadows granted north of Indian Brook, whether to Purchasers or to newcomers. None were granted in Billingsgate Meadow, presumably because there were no productive lots left, and the same seems to have been true of the Silver Spring area. Twelve new meadow lots with a total area of 25 acres were allotted along Blackfish Creek and six covering 22 acres in the Bound Brook area. A couple of grants adding up to six acres were made near Bog (Loagy) Bay and another two along "Billingsgate River" (presumably the West Arm of Duck Creek).

Nevertheless by the end of the seventeenth century a large amount of common undivided land, of which a considerable portion was meadowland, still remained within the town of Eastham. These extensive commons were giving occasion to serious problems. Trees were being cut at an increasing rate, and cattle, horses, sheep, and swine grazing at large on town lands were destroying the ground cover. In 1700 the town meeting elected Samuel Mayo senior and Joseph Doane as "agents or atturnies ... to prosecute to effect in law against any person or persons that have or shall intrude upon any of said town's common." The following year the town voted that the Indians could no longer live wherever they wished within the town's common but rather were to be confined to special areas to be allotted to them by a committee. Such developments indicate that it was becoming more and more difficult to manage and police the town's undivided land. The obvious easy answer was to distribute all the common lands among the inhabitants and let each man guard his own property. A number of years were going to be needed to carry out this solution, but a first step was taken on May 11, 1702 when it was voted "that the common meadow or hay ground belonging to the town of Eastham shall be divided to the true proprietors." For this purpose it was decided to create a committee of twelve men to make an equitable distribution. The members, duly elected on May 26, set about the task, and during 1703 and 1704 meadow lots throughout the town were granted to various inhabitants.

A number of fertile meadows lay behind coastal dunes, as at Billingsgate Meadow and near the mouth of Little River. Such meadows were at risk, for as the shores eroded the dunes migrated inland, burying the meadows behind them. Moreover when storms occurred at high tides the dunes were sometimes washed over and the meadows inundated. The flooding was even more frequent if the dunes had been broken down by grazing stock or by traffic of men and carts. These dangers were perceived even though their causes were not clearly understood, and the committee on common meadows in 1703 established a policy of compensating the owners of destroyed grasslands with meadows or other land of comparable value. In. due course such claims for compensation were made. For instance in 1710 Samuel Mayo claimed that the meadow allotted him in 1703 at the mouth of the Little River had been buried by a sand dune; in compensation he was awarded "two points of upland lying within his meadow fence at Billingsgate [Meadow]."

THE FIRST GRANTS OF UPLAND: JOHN SMALLEY AND JOB COLE

The history of the successive constructions of dwellings, barns, stores, taverns, wharves, and eventually a meeting house and the clearing of upland for cultivation is far more complex. The hamlet of Billingsgate, as it was called, was slow in developing; during the seventeenth and eighteenth centuries it consisted merely of dispersed farms mostly clustered in a number of widely separated areas. The village that was to grow up along Commercial and Main Streets was not built until the first half of the nineteenth century.

The precise or even approximate locations of seventeenth century grants are difficult to determine because of the conventions of property description practiced by the town officers, none of whom was a professional surveyor. As we have seen, the name Billingsgate was applied to all the territory from Indian Brook on the south to Bound Brook on the north. The southern portion between Indian Brook and Blackfish Creek was loosely designated as Hither Billingsgate, and the northern portion, particularly the area bordering Herring Brook between Black Pond and Williams Pond, as Farther or Yonder Billingsgate. The usage of the name "Little Billingsgate" is more difficult to pin down. It seems clear that "little" had the sense of "new," as in various English and New England place names such as Little Compton. It is possible to find instances when "Little Billingsgate" was applied to locations anywhere from Indian Brook to Bound Brook. On the other hand there was a tendency, particularly in the seventeenth century, to use the term "Little Billingsgate" for the area of the Herring River estuary below Pamet Point, referring to other areas as simply "Billingsgate."

Frequently the names of rivers, creeks, and brooks were used to locate grants, however approximately. Unfortunately for the historian many of these stream names have changed in the last three centuries. We can only guess, for instance, the locations of Coggin's and Naaman's Creeks. It seems fairly certain, however, that "Little River" was a shortened form of "Little Billingsgate River" and designated the outlet of the Herring River which then flowed into Cape Cod Bay between Bound Brook and Griffith's (Griffin) Islands and which in the nineteenth century came to be known as Duck Harbor. This usage is quite clear in land grants to Jabez Snow in 1683 and to Josiah Cook in 1695. On the other hand, a meadow grant to Samuel Hix in 1673 refers to a "Little Billingsgate River" adjacent to "the Indian Field," which from other sources we know was on the north bank of Duck Creek. This "Little Billingsgate River" must have been the same as the "Billingsgate River" named in another early grant and identical with the stream generally called in the eighteenth and nineteenth centuries the West Arm of Duck Creek and in the twentieth century Mayo's Creek.

The earliest dated grant for a twenty-acre tenement (dwelling) lot together with adjacent meadowland was that made April 20, 1659 to John Smalley, one of the original Eastham Purchasers:

> *Granted to John Smalley a parcel of meadow containing 4 acres more or less, lying at Little Billingsgate, from Job Cole's bounds which lyeth where Pamet path turns up into the woods, so west down to the creek, thence to the point at the head of the marsh*

toward the [Pamet] purchasers .... Granted to John Smalley 20 acres of upland lying at the end of Boundbrook, lying at the head of the marsh at Little Billingsgate, also 4 acres of marsh lying at a point at the eastern side of the Cranberry swamp where Pamet path turns up into the woods from there to the head of the marsh towards the above sd. upland from the southerly point of upland to the creek ....

This grant must be read together with that made to Job Cole, another Purchaser, dated March 8, 1667 but obviously laid out before Smalley's grant, for which it provided a bound:

A parcel of upland and meadow granted to Job Cole at a place called Little Billingsgate containing twenty acres of upland be it more or less, and four acres of meadow be it more or less, the upland lying on the northern side of the mouth of the river and meadow lying on the east side of the creek that runs from Little Billingsgate from the point of the Herring River to another point at the eastern side of a cranberry swamp, where Pamet path turns up into the woods, from there west down to the creek ....

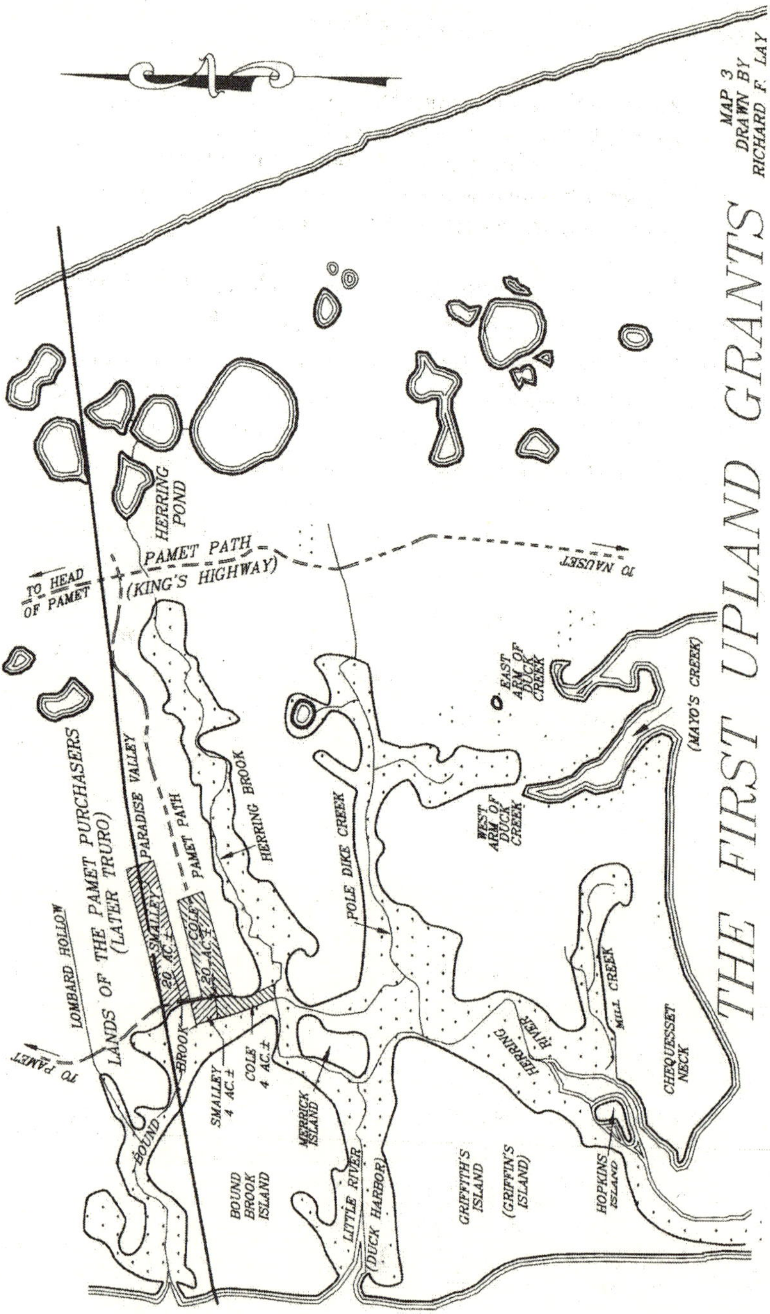
THE FIRST UPLAND GRANTS
MAP 3
DRAWN BY
RICHARD F. LAY
LANDS OF THE PAMET PURCHASERS
(LATER TRURO)
TO HEAD OF PAMET
PAMET PATH
(KING'S HIGHWAY)
TO NAUSET
HERRING POND
PARADISE VALLEY
PAMET PATH
HERRING BROOK
POLE DIKE CREEK
LOMBARD HOLLOW
TO PAMET
SMALLEY 20 AC.±
COLE 20 AC.±
SMALLEY 4 AC.±
COLE 4 AC.±
BOUND BROOK
BOUND BROOK ISLAND
MERRICK ISLAND
LITTLE RIVER
(DUCK HARBOR)
GRIFFITH'S ISLAND
(GRIFFIN'S ISLAND)
HERRING RIVER
HOPKINS ISLAND
MILL CREEK
CHEQUESSET NECK
WEST ARM OF DUCK CREEK
EAST ARM OF DUCK CREEK
(MAYO'S CREEK)

Pamet Path (whose track is now followed by Pamet Point Road and the Old County Road leading down from South Truro) led south from Pamet Harbor across the hills overlooking Cape Cod Bay, descended to skirt the edges of the marshes east of Bound Brook Island, and then turned east into the woods to ascend a hollow. From the head of the hollow it swung right toward the Herring River and followed the stream's northern bank to a point a quarter mile west of Herring Pond, where it joined the old trail and cart way going from the Head of Pamet to the Eastham meeting house. Job Cole's bound, "where Pamet path turns up into the woods," must have been at the present junction of the Old County Road and Pamet Point Road. Bound Brook flowed from springs in Paradise Valley, where Smalley had his twenty-acre grant, and emptied into Cape Cod Bay at the northwest corner of Bound Brook Island. The language of the grants indicates that Bound Brook was linked to the Herring River by a creek running north and south on the eastern edge of a cranberry bog, forming the western boundaries of Cole's and Smalley's meadow lots. (Map 3)

There is no written or archaeological proof that John Smalley built a dwelling on his twenty acres, but if he did not then his heir or assign, Thomas Mulford, certainly did, most probably on the site of the surviving cellar hole about a quarter of a mile up Paradise Valley. In the 1690s or earlier Mulford, whose family had first settled on Long Island, came into possession of Smalley's property and at the same time of Smalley's rights and privileges as a Purchaser. It is likely that he was Smalley's son-in-law.

In 1691 it was discovered that the "bound mark" which had been erected just south of the mouth of Bound Brook to establish the boundary between the lands of the Eastham Purchasers and those of the Pamet Proprietors had been lost "by reason of the seas breaking in upon the land." Consequently the Eastham town meeting commissioned Captain Jonathan Sparrow and John Doane II to erect a new monument. The commissioners took their charge to include running a new boundary line due east from the new stone. This survey not only placed the northern tip of Bound Brook Island within the lands of the Pamet Proprietors but also cut across Smalley's twenty-acre grant and put its northeastern portion within the Pamet lands. In 1695 Mulford protested and was compensated by the Eastham town meeting with the award of eight acres of adjoining common land equal in area to what he had lost.

In the same year Thomas Mulford also received, under the provisions of the Agreement of 1694 between the Eastham Purchasers and the town, six acres of meadowland extending along the south side of the Pamet boundary line from the northeast corner of Bound Brook Island to Mulford's existing property and also two more acres of upland adjoining the eight he had just received. In addition, he was granted in 1703 one and half acres of meadow at the eastern side of Bound Brook Island and in 1704 another meadow of about three-quarters of an acre adjoining the island. These details illustrate that it was possible for a person of influence and privilege to amass a sizable and presumably productive estate in real property without any investment of money.

Job Cole's twenty acres of upland lay south of the Smalley-Mulford holdings, probably extending up the narrow hollow enclosed on the south by the steep slopes of Pamet Point, beyond which the Herring River flowed from a "mouth" into the marshy basin lying between the point, Bound Brook and Merrick Islands, and Cole's Neck. There is no known written or archaeological evidence that Job Cole built a dwelling here or that he added to his holdings as Mulford did. He may have taken the land only as an investment, for he made similar acquisitions elsewhere in Eastham. In 1665 he was granted meadows on "Billingsgate River" and Blackfish Creek, and in 1677 twenty acres of upland just north of Indian Brook.

It is possible that Daniel Cole, his brother, later acquired Job's twenty acres of upland and his meadowland at Pamet Point, for in 1666 he was granted four acres of meadow at "Little Billingsgate ... adjoining to Robert Wixam ... at the turning of the [Herring} River ... at the opening of the marsh that goeth to the sea." This description seems to fit the area west and north of Merrick Island, which was near Job's original meadow grant. Moreover, Daniel also received in 1666 two grants along the bay shore of Bound Brook Island one acre in width, the first, twenty acres long, extending south from Bound Brook, and the second, ten acres long, extending north from Little River (Duck Harbor), so that the two parcels must have overlapped and included the entire western shore of Bound Brook Island.

James, John, Job, and Daniel Cole arrived in Plymouth in 1633, James coming from Saco and the other three presumably directly from England. Job married Rebecca Collier of Duxbury and moved to Yarmouth in 1642 and then in 1648 to Eastham, where he was joined by his brother Daniel. He served as constable in 1648 and 1654 and died sometime before 1694. His son, Daniel Jr., a prominent figure in Eastham, was elected the town's representative to the Court in Plymouth from 1666 to 1670 and in 1672.

GRANTS OF UPLAND ON BOUND BROOK AND GRIFFITH'S ISLANDS AND NEAR DUCK CREEK, SILVER SPRING, AND INDIAN BROOK

The twenty-acre grants to Job Cole and John Smalley in 1659 or earlier initiated the settlement of Billingsgate, beginning in "Little Billingsgate," that is, the vicinity of Pamet Point and Bound Brook and Griffith's Islands. During the 1660s six Purchasers (in addition to Smalley and Job Cole} received twenty-acre grants plus meadowland in this area; they usually appear to have actually taken possession of their lands before the recorded dates of the grants. We have already noted Daniel Cole's twenty- and ten-acre strips along the western side of Bound Brook Island. Robert Wixam's grant, postdated 1669 and 1672, of twenty acres of upland and four of meadow was on the eastern side of Bound Brook Island. In 1663 Nicholas Snow was recorded as having received "a parcel of upland, containing 20 acres more or less, at Little Billingsgate upon the Island next Little Billingsgate on the farther side of the mouth of the Herring River on the farther side of the Island next the bay bounded between Robert Wixam and Daniel Cole." This appears to have been a strip along the Cape Cod Bay shore of Griffith's Island corresponding to Daniel Cole's bayside grant on Bound Brook Island. It is possible that these shorelines were valued for the control they might have given over offshore whaling. Richard Higgins' grant, dated 1665, was for "an Island commonly so called between Coggin's creek and Naarnan's creek at Little Billingsgate with all the meadowing and sedge marsh ground adjoining thereunto on both sides the creeks." This description may have referred to what is now known as Merrick Island, and the Herring River may at that time have divided into two streams known by these (Indian?) names flowing on opposite sides of the island. The description of Edward Bang's grant, dated 1670, for twenty acres of upland and four of meadow probably referred to the southern portion of Bound Brook Island. It adjoined land belonging to John Jenkins, whose grant has not been found in the Eastham records. There is no evidence, with the exception of the Smalley land, that any of these grants was developed as a homestead; rather they appear to have been acquired as investments to be sold or held for future use by descendants.

The same was probably true of the grants received by Purchasers from the 1660s to the 1680s in the Duck Creek area. One of the earliest of these was the twenty acres of upland and four of meadow allotted to Josiah Cook in 1666 "at the head of the Cove southernmost arm of Duck Creek," abutting grants to John Freeman and Edward Bangs, also Purchasers. Neither of these two latter grants appear in surviving records. In the same year twenty acres of upland were granted jointly to John Doane senior and Daniel Cole in a strip one acre deep along the northern bank of Duck Creek. Another joint grant in the same area was that made in 1673 to Thomas Prince and John Doane senior for twenty acres of upland in a "nook at the going in of Billingsgate River [the West Arm of Duck Creek] from [the East Arm of] Duck Creek." Thomas Prince also received at the same time ten acres of upland on the northwest side of Duck Creek.

These grants on the north and west banks of Duck Creek seem to have been intended to give to the grantees control of the shoreline with a view perhaps to future construction of wharves or shipyards or other such maritime uses. The steep bluffs and hills on the western and northern banks extending northeast from the site of the future railroad tracks would not, one would think, have attracted a settler seeking arable land. Farther inland, however flat lands known as the Indian Field and Reilly's Field had probably been Indian corn fields. Other smaller grants of upland made to Purchasers in Billingsgate prior to the 1690s may have been intended for agricultural use.

A third area of early land taking was that in Hither Billingsgate inland from Silver Spring Harbor. This embayment south of Lieutenant's Island provided protection from south west and west winds in the seventeenth and early eighteenth centuries, when Billingsgate Beach and Billingsgate Point formed an unbroken barrier to the west. This small harbor, into which flowed Indian Brook, Silver Spring Brook, Fresh Brook, and several smaller streams, contained extensive oyster beds and in the seventeenth and eighteenth centuries was considerably deeper than it is today. It served the inhabitants of Eastham dwelling south of Blackfish Creek as their principal and most useful harbor for the loading and discharging of vessels. Moreover the country inland, level and well watered, was good farming land.

Richard Higgins, a Purchaser, was granted in this area sometime prior to 1672 ten acres of upland, on which he built a dwelling. Daniel Cole took title in 1666 to four acres of upland north of Indian Brook just west of the cart way that crossed the brook by a bridge. His brother Job, it will be recalled, received in 1677 twenty acres of upland on the north side of Indian Brook abutting meadows owned by William Brown, William Walker, and John Mayo. Later, in 1698, Isaac Doane was granted four acres on Indian Brook and acquired additional adjoining land in 1711 and 1715.

Thus by the early decades of the eighteenth century what might be called a small hamlet had grown up in the vicinity of Silver Spring and Silver Spring Brook. It never had any local name other than Hither Billingsgate, but it was given surprising prominence on eighteenth-century maps. The importance of Silver Spring Harbor for vessels sailing to the Lower Cape was such that it came to the notice of the English cartographer Thomas Jeffereys when he was preparing in 1755 the first edition of his map entitled *Most Inhabited Part of New* England, the earliest largescale map of New England. Jeffereys assumed – not unreasonably – that the existence of a Silver Spring Harbor implied a town named Silver Spring, which he therefore carefully placed on his map next to the harbor. This imaginary town continued to appear on subsequent editions of Jeffereys' map until the end of the century and also on other European maps derived from Jeffereys. It is not found, however, in the Carleton map of 1796 published in Boston, which superseded Jeffereys and was compiled from local New England sources. The sketch map made by a Wellfleet committee in 1795 for Carleton's information showed Silver Spring Harbor but of course no town or hamlet of that name.

THE AGREEMENT OF 1694

As we have noted, until 1694 the town meeting granted upland in Billingsgate suitable for the siting of dwellings only to the Purchasers and their heirs. Insofar as the town records indicate only two of these grants, those made to John Smalley and Richard Higgins, were developed as homesteads. It is probable, however, that squatters had appropriated common land in Billingsgate without permission from the town meeting and had erected dwellings. It is also probable that other newcomers, acting legally, had bought land in Billingsgate from Purchasers. The local historian Enoch Pratt (who relied largely on oral sources and who is not always trustworthy) listed as living in Billingsgate before 1670 the following newcomers: Henry Atkins, Samuel Atkins, George Crisp, William Dyer, Moses Hatch, Thomas Newcomb, John Smith, George Ward, and John Witherell; and as arriving between 1670 and 1700: Isaac Baker, Nathaniel Covel, John Rich, and John Yates. Of these we know that George Crisp and John Yates received meadow grants in Billingsgate in 1659 or earlier.

Despite these concessions, during the last decades of the seventeenth century a considerable amount of pressure must have been exerted on the Purchasers in an effort to induce them to make grants of common land for house lots to younger sons and to acceptable newcomers. We do not know what form this pressure took, but clearly it did exist. On

August 1, 1694 an Agreement was signed by the fourteen "Town Purchasers": Ensign Jonathan Bangs (heir to Edward Bangs); Daniel Cole senior; Daniel Cole junior (heir to Job Cole); Josiah Cook; John Doane II (heir to John Doane I); Major John Freeman; Samuel Freeman (on behalf of Thomas Prince); Jonathan Higgins (heir to Richard Higgins); Samuel Hix; John Jenkins; Thomas Mulford (heir or assign of John Smalley); John Rogers (heir to Joseph Rogers); Mark Snow (heir to Nicholas Snow); and Titus Wixam (heir to Robert Wixam).

They and their predecessors (these men formally agreed) "appearing to be the real purchasers of the lands within the township of Eastham of the natives," established a committee of "five or seven" "negative men" with the power to veto any land grant made by the town meeting and furthermore agreed "that the said Major John Freeman, Ensign Bangs, Mark Snow and the rest of the above named, in consideration above said, do accept of, for [themselves] and [their] heirs, all the allowed inhabitants of the town of Eastham to be joint proprietors with [them] in all the undivided lands and the great island at Billingsgate within the township of Eastham ... only therein reserving to [themselves] liberty . . . within a year after the date hereof to lay out to [themselves] 8 acres of land apiece where [they might] make choice of in the undivided lands from the northerly side of Great Blackfish river [to] the bounds between the Town and Pamet purchasers, the neck called James' Neck at Billingsgate, and the great Island aforesaid at Billingsgate only excepted."

There are a number of remarkable and significant provisions in this Agreement of 1694. Perhaps the most important is the concept of the "allowed inhabitant." Hitherto, it appears, certain worthy newcomers such as Richard Sparrow and Captain Jonathan Sparrow had been accepted as men worthy of appointment to important offices and committees and presumably they had been permitted to vote in town meetings, but the town records show no formal actions conferring on them status comparable to that of the Purchasers. After 1694, however, it became the practice, starting in 1702, to vote formally that certain men "be taken in for townsmen of Eastham." The new "allowed inhabitants" were both younger sons and grandsons of Town Purchasers and also members of new families destined to play important roles in the histories of Eastham and Billingsgate, the Youngs, the Mayos, the Collinses, the Knowles, and the Smiths, as well as members of families that failed to take root. This principle of the allowed inhabitant was to serve for centuries to give to the people of Eastham and Wellfleet, as was indeed the effect in other towns, the perception of themselves as members of a corporation of coproprietors of common resources.

It is also important to note the reserved areas from which the Purchasers could not elect to receive their eight acres. James' Neck, today called Indian Neck, had been reserved, as we know, since the purchase of Billingsgate from the Punonakanits for the exclusive use of the Indians. Great Island was common land used by the inhabitants for the landing of whales and the trying of blubber over fires fueled with wood cut on the island. It was not divided into private lots until 1715. Not mentioned because it was south of Blackfish Creek was a third reserved area, Lieutenant's Island, not to be open to grants to individuals until 1704.

Not all the fourteen Purchasers took advantage of their rights to eight acres in Billingsgate. Samuel Freeman did not do so on behalf of Thomas Prince, nor did Daniel Cole junior, the son of the deceased Job Cole, nor did Titus Wixam, son of Robert Wixam. For some reason Jonathan Bangs received the allotment of John Jenkins instead of that of his father, Edward Bangs, and both Jonathan Rogers and John Rogers, sons of Joseph Rogers, received eight acres each. Probably a market in these shares developed.

It was decided that the eight-acre allotments should each be divided into six acres of meadow and two acres of upland. The choices made may serve to give us some ideas on the kinds of land in Billingsgate that were thought valuable. Of the eleven Purchasers who actually received land, four (Mark Snow, Daniel Cole senior, Josiah Cook, and John Jenkins) requested parcels adjoining one another along the high banks or "clifts" between Duck Creek and James' Neck, each 57 poles deep and 7 poles wide along the bank (940.5 x 115.5 feet), extending north from the point where access to James' Neck began. Titus Wixam already held the fifth and northernmost of these contiguous lots. The value of this waterside land is not obvious but it seems likely that this was thought a good place to build wharves in the future, and indeed one of these parcels was later to be the site of Enterprise Wharf, built in 1837. Jonathan Rogers also preferred Duck Creek shoreline but for a different reason, electing to receive six acres of meadow and two of upland behind a cove called Stumpy Meadow. He was no doubt seeking the best unclaimed meadowland still available, as were other Purchasers: Josiah Cook and John Jenkins at Little River; Mark Snow behind James' Neck; and Daniel Cole on the southwest side of the Herring River near its mouth. Others elected to extend previous grants: John Doane chose eight acres of sedge meadow on Chequesset Neck (by then also known as Doane's Neck) and Thomas Mulford, as has been noted, took two acres of upland near the head of Bound Brook and six acres of meadow along the Pamet Proprietors' line. Still others made choices with views of opening up new areas: Jonathan Higgins at the northeast corner of Griffith's Island, John Rogers at the southern and southwest corners of Griffith's Island, and Samuel Hix and John Freeman upland and meadow on both sides of Herring Brook between its source in Herring Pond and the point near Black Pond where it enters the marsh. The two-acre upland lot that John Freeman chose on the south bank of the brook just east of the ford where the cart way crossed the stream was to be the site of a Freeman house which still stands today.

YEARS OF GROWTH, 1694-1715

The effect of the Agreement of 1694 was to increase rapidly the number of dwellings and homesteads in Billingsgate. Newcomers from various parts of the Province of Massachusetts (to which the Plymouth Colony was annexed in 1692) had, as we have seen, been settling on common lands without permission. At least two of them, John Callens (or Collings) in 1698 and John Swett (or Sweat or Sweet) in 1700, received grants of five and seven acres respectively, which were described in both cases as located "where his dwelling now stands."

We have seen that grants were made on Bound Brook Island as early as the 1660s, but it was not until the early 1700s that the actual settlement of the island began. Stephen Atwood II received grants on the south side of the island of five acres of upland in 1700 and of an additional adjoining seven acres in 1704. Later, in 1715, Eleazer Atwood, his son, received twelve acres "on the northerly side of his former plain lot" (perhaps conveyed by his father) and in addition an acre on the north side of the island adjoining a meadow he had purchased from Thomas Mulford. Joshua, another of Stephen Atwood's sons, also received in 1715 nine acres on the island on the north side of his plain lot, the grant or conveyance of which does not appear in surviving records. Similarly one James Brown seems to have acquired by some unrecorded means land on the island, for in 1715 he was granted an additional adjoining parcel.

During the same years settlements were being made in other parts of Billingsgate. In the Duck Creek area Eldad Atwood, a brother of Stephen, had earlier bought a parcel originally granted to the Purchaser Joseph Rogers on what was then called Rogers' Neck at the head of Duck Creek near Hawes' Pond. Now in 1703 he received a grant of meadow, sedge, and hay ground augmenting the original Rogers grant. In the same vicinity Elisha Eldridge received in 1709 two and a half acres of upland "near" Duck Creek, and John Myrick was granted the following year three adjoining acres. In Hither Billingsgate William Brown was granted five acres of upland on the north side of Indian Brook in 1700 and Samuel Brown received in 1710 three acres of upland on the north side of Blackfish Creek.

THE LAND DIVISIONS OF 1711 AND 1715

By 1711 the pressures of population growth and the difficulty of managing and policing the common lands had made it imperative that the remaining undivided upland be distributed equitably among the allowed inhabitants, just as in 1702 it had been necessary to divide the remaining common meadowlands. A town meeting met on March 26 to act on the matter, and it appointed a committee consisting of Daniel

Cole, Joseph Collins senior, John Doane III, Samuel Knowles, John Paine, and Micajah Snow to draw up a plan for land distribution. They proposed that every male allowed inhabitant twenty-one years of age or older be granted four acres of "open or plain land," or more if necessary "for quality," and that a committee be chosen to lay out the allotted lands, subject to the approval of the majority of the "Negative Men," as provided in the Agreement of 1694.

Then on May 21 of the same year it was further voted that four acres of woodland were to be granted "to each proper tenement within the town, that is to say, where there is a house and land belonging thereunto," with extra acreage for two families living on one farm or in one tenement, and in addition six acres of woodland to each male person. The allotments were to be increased as necessary to make the shares equal in quality.

Finally at this same momentous meeting, it was voted that Great Island in Billingsgate was to be divided into twenty-four sections and that each allowed inhabitant was to have an equal share in one of these parcels as determined by a drawing of lots. The committee named to lay out the island consisted of John Cole junior, Lieutenant John Doane, Joseph Doane Esq., Thomas Doane, Captain Samuel Freeman, John Knowles, Mr. Isaac Pepper, and John Young.

This wholesale distribution of common lands by the town meeting met with considerable opposition in Billingsgate from both the local English settlers and the Indians. On June 12, 1711 twenty-five English met and drew up a petition to Governor Joseph Dudley to prevent the division of common lands in Billingsgate. Likewise twenty Indians signed a similar petition, which was accompanied by a covering letter signed by John Doane III of Billingsgate. Both the English and the Indians were accustomed to using the common lands as sources of wood and for grazing stock, and the Indians since time immemorial had gathered on these lands bark, berries, and other wild resources. These protests were, however, without effect.

In 1715 in a series of meetings the town of Eastham voted to take further action to divide among the inhabitants common uplands, meadows, and marshes. A committee of proprietors composed of John Collins, Joseph Doane, John Knowles, Jonathan Linnell, Nathaniel Mayo, and Jonathan Young were elected to divide the remaining common land into plain lots and wood lots; and a second committee, composed of John Cole junior, Joseph Doane, Thomas Doane, Samuel Freeman, Jonathan Higgins, and John Knowles was elected to allot the various parcels conveniently to the grantees.

In this division a total of 143 allotments were laid out, each usually consisting of two or more parcels. Twenty-four allotments, ranging in area from four to twenty acres, were made north of Indian Brook in Billingsgate. The type or types of land were not specified; presumably each grantee received a mixture of upland, meadow, and marsh, but probably not of good woodland. These allotments indicate the expansion of settlements in various localities: grants to Eleazer Atwood, Joshua Atwood, James Brown, and William Brown on Bound Brook Island; to Joseph Atkins, John Atwood, John Doane III, Daniel Mayo, Samuel Mayo, and Samuel Smith in the Chequesset Neck area; to Elisha Cole and William Cole on Cole's Neck; to Isaac Doane near Indian Brook; to John Mulford at the head of Bound Brook; to Samuel Brown, Abiah Harding, and Samuel Harding near Blackfish Creek; and to Eleazer Cole at the head of Duck Creek.

In addition, 156 new wood lots were granted throughout the town, including a proportionate number in Billingsgate.

In this same year, 1715, was carried out the division of Great Island, already voted in May of 1711. As had been authorized, the island was divided into twenty-four strips and joint ownership of each of these sections was granted to five or six allowed inhabitants. The total number of grantees was 135. Since the island had hitherto been common land, whaling boats manned by inhabitants had been free to bring blackfish or other whales ashore anywhere on its beaches and to try the blubber over fires. As the supply of wood dwindled, however, the equitable distribution of the timber still standing had become a pressing problem. This parceling out of ownership of the island apparently seemed a fair solution. Furthermore the town meeting had voted in 1711 that lot owners were to be free to pass over one another's land to cart wood and water to their "whale houses," in which they tried the blubber. The same problem had existed on Lieutenant's Island, where whales were likewise brought ashore to be cut up, and a similar solution had been found in 1704, when it was voted no longer to reserve the island for the support of the minister but to open it up to private grants.

While this division of Great Island may have prevented confrontations between whaling parties it also resulted in the swift destruction of all the trees on the island and consequently the abandonment of the island by offshore whalers. The only possible use of the denuded ground was as a pasture for horses, cattle, and sheep, but the overgrazing that ensued destroyed the ground cover and exposed the thin topsoil to the onshore winds. Soon the once verdant island was turned into a great dune.

It has been supposed from archaeological evidence and from oral tradition that Samuel Smith maintained during the late seventeenth and early eighteenth centuries on the northeast corner of Great Island a tavern where he provided lodging, food, and drink for whaling men. The excavated foundation must date, however, from a time considerably later than 1715. Smith was not even one of the allowed inhabitants permitted to participate in the Great Island lottery in 1715. Later, it is true, he did buy up many shares in the lots, which had become virtually worthless, and he claimed at one time to be the principal landholder of the island. The earliest evidence of his ownership, however, is a petition he and John Holbrook presented to the General Court in 1742 in support of a bill to regulate the grazing of stock on the island. As we shall see in Chapter IV, the supposed tavern must have been built in 1749 or later, ceramic and pipe-stem archaeological evidence to the contrary notwithstanding.[6]

THE INDIAN LANDS

The extensive division of common lands in 1715 required the resolution of the problem of Indian lands, particularly in Billingsgate. The estimated one hundred Punonakanit Indians living around the harbor in 1620 were survivors of the epidemic that ravaged the Indians of Massachusetts around 1615, having been caused by contacts with whites. Though undoubtedly reduced from their earlier numbers, the Punonakanits do not appear to have suffered as grievously as did the villages around Plymouth and elsewhere on the mainland. The Indian Neck ossuary indicates that this area had long been the site of a year-round vlllage.[7] and there is archaeological evidence of other settlements or temporary camps around the entire perimeter of the harbor and on Griffith's Island, Cole's Neck, and elsewhere.

In spite of the influx of the English the local Indians seem to have survived fairly well through the seventeenth century. Daniel Gookin reported that in 1674 the combined population of Punonakanit and Meeshawn (the Pamet and North Pamet groups) was seventy-two adults plus an undetermined number of children. This total may be compared with Gookin's figures for the same year of forty-four adults in Potanumaquut (Harwich and Pleasant Bay) and seventy-one adults in Manamoyick (Chatham).[8] In 1685 Governor Hinkley estimated that in Pamet (Meeshawn), Billingsgate, and Eastham or Nauset there were a total of 264 adults and more than three times as many children under twelve.[9] On the authority of Samuel Treat, the minister at Eastham, who zealously served the Lower Cape Indians, the missionaries Grimal Rawson and Samuel Danforth estimated in 1698 that East Harbor (Meeshawn), Billingsgate, Eastham, Monomoy, and Harwich together contained five hundred Indians. At East Harbor and Billingsgate Daniel Munshe was the Indian preacher and Daniel Samuel the Indian ruler. These two allied villages, it was reported, contained about twenty houses, some sheltering two families.[10] Like the other Indians of the Lower Cape, the Punonakanits subscribed in 1671 to a treaty of alliance with the government of New Plymouth and remained neutral during King Philip's War, 1675-1678. Thus, in summary, the evidence is that until about 1700 the Indians of Billingsgate more or less maintained their numbers and existed on peaceful terms with the English, continuing to dwell on the common lands, part of which had been expressly reserved for their use.

There were, however, signs of competition for resources, as we have already noted. In 1674 it was agreed in town meeting to apprehend persons from other towns caught taking oysters or oyster shells from Billingsgate Bay. Then in 1691 it was voted "that no person or persons shall cutt any wood or timber upon any of the town's commons that is not granted to any person; so as to convey or transport it out of the town." Again in 1695: "The Selectmen ... taking into serious consideration the great damage which doth accrue to the town by reason of persons cutting cord wood and timber upon the commons and transporting it out of the township ... doe order and enact that from and after the tenth day of April next ensuing ... NO [sic] person or persons whatsoever shall cut any wood or timber whatsoever upon any of the town's or individual land within the township of Eastham other than that [sic] what shall be improved within the same." In 1710 the town meeting ordered the selectmen to petition the General Court concerning "foreigners" fetching oysters from Billingsgate.

How many of these intruders and "foreigners" were English and how many were Indians we do not know, but it is significant that in 1701 the town "voted that the foreign Indians be not suffered to live on the town's common, and that these Indians that are natives of the town shall be confined to live at such places as the town shall order. Mr. Samuel Treat, Captain Jonathan Sparrow, Mr. John Doane, and Mr. Samuel Knowles were chosen to lay out places for the Indians to live upon." Finally, in 1711 when the town came to grips with the need to distribute equitably the common land, it voted "to consider and propose what is proper to be done with reference to the Indians in respect of allowing them any privilege for wood &c., when the commons come to be divided."

Carrying out this resolution, on April 14, 1715 the town voted "that before said [common] lands are all divided there shall be a certain parcell or parcells of wood land laid out ... for the use and benefit of such Indians as are the proper natives of the town, to set their houses on and for fire wood ... in such place or places as may be convenient for the Indians and least prejudicial to the English." The lands were to be granted in the names of certain leading Indians, who would receive them on behalf of all their people. Moreover it was stipulated that these lands could not be alienated without a formal vote by the proprietors of the town. At a second town meeting on September 24, 1716 the nominal grantees were designated: Pepeas Frances; Frances Frances; James Mark; Sam Tripp alias Tuis; and Nacan Jones alias Abram Jones. To them were allotted four tracts.

The most important was that which the Indians had already reserved (and which according to them had never been sold to the English), James' Neck. It consisted of all the upland of the peninsula now known as Indian Neck (but not the meadow and marsh lying between the neck and the mainland), beginning at a north-south line across the narrow barrier beach linking the neck to the mainland. This reservation provided the Indians with a fresh water supply at the marsh known as Sewell's Gutter and access to rich shellfish. beds in Chipman's Cove and indeed all the way around the neck to Field Point, but it probably comprised little meadowland or upland suitable for cultivating corn or other crops.

The other parcels granted to the Indians were smaller. Two, of 14 3/4 and five acres, were located just south of Fresh Brook in Hither Billingsgate. A third of two acres was north of John Paine's dwelling, probably in the vicinity of the Eastham meeting house.

Though the English were perhaps sincere in their professed intent to make land grants "as may be convenient for the Indians and least prejudicial to the English," there was clearly no thought of allotting land to the Indians on the same basis "as to quantity and quality" as to the English inhabitants. The fact is that the Indians were being subjected to heavy economic pressures. Deprived of access to the common, on which they had always depended for wood, food, and various other resources such as bark, without arable land and wood lots, unable to make a living and without marketable skills except whaling, the Indian population was reduced to poverty and probably malnutrition and disease. Their mortality rate rose, particularly during the smallpox epidemic of 1746-1748, and their numbers declined proportionately. In 1734, for reasons which were not recorded but which one may guess, the town voted to exchange the Indian lands on James' Neck for some property that Samuel Smith offered in trade, "as the negative men shall judge equivalent to that in said James his Neck." Later it was voted that John Paine could exchange land for the Indian land near his dwelling.

It is clear that during the course of the eighteenth century, in distinct contrast to the preceding years, the Indians were a declining minority existing with difficulty in a state of economic, social, and political inferiority. Their status was dramatically symbolized by the rough stones with crudely scratched initials and dates marking their graves in a segregated area in the rear of the Chequesset Neck cemetery. Kittredge estimated that in 1764 there were eleven Indians living in Wellfleet and four in Eastham, and by 1792 those in Wellfleet had been reduced to three or four women and a man, who lived to the north of Pamet Point Road. It has been said that the last Billingsgate Indian was a woman named Delilah Gibbs, who died sometime after 1838. A family named Kinnecum, however, perhaps of mixed blood, lived in the vicinity of Gull Pond and Kinnacum Pond and continued into the twentieth. century, the last local descendant dying in 1959.

THE KING'S HIGHWAY

As the settlement of Billingsgate increased so did the network of sand roads connecting the various sections of the hamlet. In 1721, probably after prompting by the county, the Eastham town meeting voted to lay out a forty-foot highway, to be known as the King's Highway or Common Road, from the Harwich line at the head of Namskaket to the Truro boundary. Though the route was described in the recorded article, mainly by references to dwellings along the way, there was nothing resembling a survey. In fact the vote did nothing more than give an official status to the cart way and former Pamet Path which already led north from Namskaket along the western side of the Town Cove to the old cemetery, veered in a northwesterly direction to go between Herring Pond and the Mill Pond and past the new meeting house, and then swung to the right to pass the Salt Pond and the Halfway Ponds. Thence the road skirted the heads of Blackfish Creek and Duck Creek and continued northward to cross Herring Brook on the west side of the lot granted to John Freeman in 1695 – in 1721 the site of Ebenezer Freeman's dwelling. From there the road ran in a northerly direction to cross the Truro line and eventually swung around the head of the Pamet River close to the Backside beach. From grant and deed descriptions we know that in many places there were two or more generally parallel ways, and the "King's Highway" shifted from one to the other by informal consensus. Moreover, as was true of all sand roads on Cape Cod, when certain stretches became too soft for easy going impatient drivers created detours which in time became permanent rights of way.

THE LAND DIVISIONS OF 1743

As we shall see in the next chapter, by the end of the first quarter of the eighteenth century the town of Eastham had been divided into three precincts or parishes, the north precinct including all of Billingsgate and the south precinct comprising what is now the town of Orleans. This political and ecclesiastical division suggested a similar decentralization of the process of allotting common lands. Consequently at the town meeting of July 6, 1743 it was voted to grant to the qualified inhabitants of the north, middle, and south parishes exclusive proprietorship of all the common lands remaining within their respective boundaries. This action regionalized, simplified, and accelerated the final division of the common. After the allotments made at the subsequent precinct meetings there was little or no common land left, save whatever may have been overlooked in the imprecise boundary descriptions or parcels that had reverted to the town by tax delinquency. The following list of qualified inhabitants of the north precinct (Billingsgate) gives an official and probably fairly accurate count of the property owners twenty-one years of age or old dwelling north of Indian Brook:

James Atkins
Eliezer [Eleazer] Atwood
Elmer Atwood
James Atwood
Jesse Atwood
John Atwood
Richard Atwood
William Atwood
Benjamin Brown
David Brown, Jr.
George Brown
Jesse Brown
Joseph Brown
Joshua Brown
Samuel Brown
William Brown
William Brown, Jr.
Daniel Cole, Jr.
Elisha Cole
Elisha Cole, Jr.
William Cole
Barnabas Cook
Benjamin Cook
Joshua Cook
Richard Cook 3d
Elisha Doane
Isaac Doane
Joseph Doane, Jr.
Ebenezer Freeman
Ebenezer Freeman [sic]
Edward Freeman
Abiah Harding
Ezekiel Harding
Isaac Harding
John Harding
Joseph Harding
Seth Harding
Thomas Higgins, Jr.
Daniel Mayo
Daniel Mayo, Jr.
Jeremiah Mayo
Samuel Mayo
Zoeth Smith
Silvenus Snow
John Treat
Nathaniel Treat
John Walker
John Walker, Jr.
Joshua Walker
Samuel Walker
Barnabas Young
Benjamin Young
Enos Young
Israel Young
Israel Young, Jr.
John Young
Jonathan Young
Jonathan Young, Jr.
Levy Young
Nathaniel Young
Stephen Young

It is interesting to note that only the four Coles, the four Cooks, the three Doanes, the three Freemans, the one Higgins, and the one Snow – a total of 16 or 26% of the allowed inhabitants of the precinct – were descendants of the original fourteen Purchasers, who had settled in Nauset less than a hundred years before.

Chapter II

From Hamlet to Parish

SQUIRE JOHN DOANE

The development of Billingsgate from a scattering of isolated dwellings into an organized community was in large part shaped by the ambitions of John Doane III and his redoubtable wife Hannah. The first John Doane, Squire Doane's grandfather, was a man of about forty when in 1630 he arrived in New Plymouth. Soon his capacity for leadership became apparent, and he was named a deacon in 1634 and an assistant to the governor in 1636. A member of the committee instructed to explore Nauset in 1644 and one of the original seven Purchasers of Eastham, he established a homestead on the north side of Nauset Marsh and acquired extensive holdings in Nauset, Pochet, Rock Harbor, and Billingsgate. On five occasions he served as the town's deputy to the Court at Plymouth. Upon his death in 1685 the leadership of the family passed to his oldest son, John II, born in Plymouth around 1635, who was a selectman of Eastham almost every year from 1678 to 1700 besides serving as constable, negative man, and deputy to both the Plymouth Colony Court and, after 1691, to the General Court of Massachusetts.

John III, born in 1664 and raised in the shadows of two such sires, with little chance of building up an estate until the death of his father, sought his fortune in Boston. There he established himself as a distiller and was successful in amassing a considerable fortune. He took as his first wife in 1686 Mehitabel Scudder, by whom he had a son, John IV, who became a mariner and died in 1723. Left a young widower, he married sometime before 1696 Hannah Hobart (1666-1731) of Hingham, niece of the Reverend Peter Hobart of that town. She bore him two sons,

Joshua, born in 1696, and Solomon, born in 1698. Soon after this second marriage he seems to have reached the decision that he had acquired enough money and real estate to satisfy amply his wants and that the moment had come to return to his origins and to create for himself a place in the burgeoning province of Massachusetts, to which Eastham and the rest of the Plymouth Colony had been annexed in 1692. Rather than return to the side of his still active father, he chose, however, to create for himself a place in a new and separate community, Billingsgate.

He therefore persuaded his father to turn over to him in anticipation of his inheritance a large tract of upland, sedge meadow, and salt meadow on Chequesset Neck. Here he built, probably around 1697, what he later described as "a double house two stories high" with a nearby gristmill and no doubt various barns and outbuildings. He also owned one or more vessels which anchored off Chequesset Neck. Archaeological research indicates that an early-eighteenth-century or late-seventeenth-century dwelling stood near the southeast corner of the Chequesset Neck cemetery; this may well have been the Doane house.

Until his father died in 1708 John Doane III held no public office and appears to have shown little interest in the affairs of the town or the hamlet. His first move toward leadership was to organize the Indians and English of Billingsgate in 1711 in their protests to Governor Dudley against the division of common lands. Two years later he was appointed justice of the peace, an office he was to hold until 1732. At the same time he began to work for the establishment of a church in Billingsgate.

THE PARTITION OF EASTHAM

These were years in which new and disruptive forces were rising in Barnstable County and in other parts of Massachusetts, fragmenting established towns and creating new ones. Eastham had, as we have seen, reached its greatest territorial expansion in 1674, when the constablewick of Eastham stretched from the Yarmouth line to Cape

Head. So extended an area could not, of course, be governed from a single meeting house. Indeed the Proprietors of Pamet (most of whom had come from Eastham) had been virtually a self-governing community since the 1650s and, as has been noted, had erected a stone bound to set off clearly their lands from those of the Eastham Purchasers. Nevertheless the Pamet lands remained legally part of Eastham, however little the Proprietors benefited from this dependency. This was obviously an unsatisfactory political organization. Consequently on May 26, 1702 the Eastham town meeting voted "that the inhabitants of Palmet [sic] shall be freed from having any part of the town charges arising in the town of Eastham, except what is to pay the Representative [to the General Court] annually, and Countie and Province rates, only the town rate already agreed upon to be made, they are to pay half what is their just proportion-always provided that they keep and support a gospel Minister among themselves."

On February 8, 1703, less than a year later, the Eastham town meeting voted to "approve of the inhabitants of Palmet who live to the Northward of the bounds of the land belonging to the town of Eastham their design to be a township if the General Court shall see cause to grant it." Two years later, however, on March 21, 1705, Pamet still continuing within the government of Eastham, the Eastham town meeting voted that three selectmen should be chosen by the inhabitants of Eastham and two by the Proprietors of Pamet.

Later in the same year, 1705, the General Court finally settled the matter by authorizing that the area north of Bound Brook be incorporated as the District of Dangerfield, and in 1709 it passed an act making the district a town by the name of Truro. Soon after, Truro was itself divided, Provincetown becoming a separate precinct in 1714 and a town in 1727. Meanwhile Eastham lost more territory on the south when in 1712 Manamoyick was incorporated as the town of Chatham.

The first move toward the secession of Billingsgate was made by the Eastham town meeting in 1700 when it voted "that all those persons that live to the North of Great Blackfish River belonging to this town, if they will hire and keep on their own cost and charge a suitable person to keep school among themselves to teach their children to read the English Bible, shall be free from paying to the town school so long as they keep one of their own." This was not an option that the people of Billingsgate were to take until after 1763, but the vote did at least establish the principle, which was to be followed later, of self-support and self-government for Billingsgate. The proposal offered in 1700 not having been implemented, however, the town meeting voted in 1705 that the schoolmaster should teach for three months "in the neighborhood of town," four months in "Pocha" (Pochet), two months about the head of the Cove, three months at the Halfway Ponds, and three months at Little Billingsgate.

Then in March 1710 it was voted that "the town of Eastham will free the Inhabitants of Billingsgate (that is, all that live to the northward of Great Blackfish Crick) from bearing any charge in supporting the minister or schoolmaster within said town, provided (and so long as) they are provided with and support an orthodox preacher to dispense the word of God unto them, and keep a writing and reading schoolmaster among them."

A few days later the town meeting further voted that in both Pochet and Billingsgate ten acres of ordinary land and ten acres of woodland were to be set aside for the benefit and support of a minister in each of these sections of the town whenever one was chosen.

THE FIRST MINISTRY OF JOSIAH OAKES

Squire Doane, as he had now come to be known, attempted to take advantage of this offer by bringing to Billingsgate a preacher, one Mr. Latimer, who did not, unfortunately, remain long. The Squire had more success, however, with his second candidate, Josiah Oakes. This young man of twenty-five was the son of Thomas Oakes, a graduate of Harvard College in 1662, physician, representative for Boston in the General Court, and speaker of the House from 1689 to 1707. In 1690 Thomas Oakes had been sent with Elisha Cooke to London to support Increase

Mather in an unsuccessful effort to obtain from William IIII the restoration of the old charter of the Massachusetts Bay Colony. Josiah, like his father, had been a student at Harvard College and had continued his studies after being graduated in order to qualify in 1711 for the M.A. degree, the usual prerequisite for a young man of the province destined for the ministry. He was invited to accept a call to the pulpit in Needham, but he refused the offer and, perhaps hesitant about his vocation, drifted for a time without a clear objective. Then in 1714 the John Doanes, who maintained their Boston connections, persuaded Josiah to preach in Billingsgate, which he did intermittently for several years, returning to Boston after each visit. Eventually early in 1718 he apparently made the decision to settle in Billingsgate permanently, bringing to the hamlet his father, then seventy-four and retired from public life. No doubt as an encouragement, John Doane, Isaac Baker, Israel Young, and perhaps others joined together as "proprietors" to build for Oakes' use a small meeting house, according to tradition twenty by twenty feet square. An archaeological dig has indicated that the building was probably located in the northwest corner of the burying ground that John Doane had laid out on Chequesset Neck in 1716 for the graves of his son Joshua, drowned in November 1716 while sailing from Rock Harbor to Billingsgate, and of Joshua's young wife Mary, who had died the preceding July. After his arrival Oakes preached regularly from the pulpit of this modest structure. He was what was known as a lay preacher, not having received a call from an established congregation and not having been regularly ordained by ministers from other parishes. It appears that Josiah and his father lived in the Doanes' house, as Josiah no doubt had done during his previous stays. This was not, as we shall see, an insignificant detail.

EASTHAM'S CALL TO SAMUEL OSBORN

Perhaps one of the circumstances that persuaded Josiah to commit himself to Billingsgate was the death in March 1717 of Samuel Treat, the beloved and respected minister to both Indians and English in Eastham since 1673. It does not appear from any evidence or from the course of events that there was any expectation that Oakes might be chosen as Treat's successor in the Eastham pulpit, though he was well qualified for the call by education. It is probable, however, that Treat's decease created new circumstances in which the establishment of a separate parish in Billingsgate with a permanent minister became a likely eventuality.

A series of town meetings were held in the Eastham meeting house devoted to the problem of Treat's replacement and to plans to build one or two new meeting houses, for the original structure near the Town Cove was seriously dilapidated and was not conveniently located for many of the inhabitants. The eventual decision was to divide the town of Eastham south of Billingsgate into two parishes to be separated by a line through Jeremiah's Gutter, a marshy inlet near the southern end of the Town Cove (approximately the present Eastham-Orleans boundary) and to build two new meeting houses, one for a new southern parish in Pochet and the other, to be built "a little to the northward of the Herring Pond Field," replacing the old meeting house near the Town Cove. Furthermore it was decided that the first minister ordained would be free to choose either of the two parishes, and that when the second meeting house was built the second minister would be called. Both meeting houses were to be built and both ministers were to be paid entirely at the expense of the middle and southern parishes, and the inhabitants of Billingsgate were to be exempt from any charges.

The search for the first minister proved difficult. It was voted in April 1717 to pay the schoolmaster, Nehemiah Hobart (a relative of Hannah Doane), to serve temporarily as minister, but he refused to accept the position permanently. The Reverend William Hubbard also declined. Harvard College, for unspecified reasons, failed to recommend a candidate. Finally in May 1718, more than a year after Treat's death, the church offered the pulpit to one Samuel Osborn, a schoolmaster teaching in Plymouth, not a Harvard graduate, and a man about whose qualifications some had serious reservations.

It may seem surprising that the deacons of Eastham had such difficulty in finding an interested candidate and that Oakes with his Harvard M.A.

did not offer himself. The fact is that the two ministries open in Eastham were not of a sort to appeal to a well qualified young candidate beginning his ecclesiastical career, and much less to a more mature man. The pessimistic predictions about the resources of Nauset made by the committee of 1644 were already being verified. Lacking an adequate harbor, its supply of wood already seriously depleted and not renewable except by ship from Maine, its limited agricultural land already suffering from overgrazing and erosion, Eastham did not have the economic base to support three ministers.

THE BILLINGSGATE PETITION OF 1718

Instead of competing for the pulpit in Pochet or in the old meeting house, Josiah Oakes, certainly with the backing of John Doane, on June 10, 1718 presented jointly with his father, the former Speaker of the House, a petition to the General Court "for that part of the Town of Eastham called Billingsgate ... praying that they may be set off and constituted a distinct Township," extending from the bounds of Truro south to Indian Brook, easterly to the sea, and westerly to the mouth of Billingsgate Bay – the very boundaries that were eventually to define the town of Wellfleet. Three days before, John Doane and Samuel Brown of Billingsgate had presented a similar petition to the Eastham town meeting. The records of that meeting of June 7 tersely describe what must have been a charged session: "Which said petition was at said meeting several times read, and the question being asked by the moderator, whether the town would grant the prayer of said petition, it passed in the negative." The bill before the General Court, which provided that the name of the new town was to be Poole and that the whaling and oyster fisheries were to be held in common by the two towns, was passed by the Council but encountered strong opposition in the House of Representatives, largely because of vigorous lobbying by John Paine, the Eastham agent at the General Court.

In view of the town meeting's repeated expressions of willingness that the inhabitants of Billingsgate be permitted to hire and support their own schoolmaster and minister and be free of assessments for the new meeting houses at Herring Pond and Pochet and for the salaries of the two new ministers to fill these pulpits, it seems most likely that the people of Eastham would have acquiesced to the establishment of a new parish and meeting house in Billingsgate, as was readily permitted for Pochet, provided there was no formal political separation. Such an arrangement would have been acceptable especially if the southern boundary of the new parish had been Blackfish Creek, for several families in Hither Billingsgate had no wish to leave the church being relocated at Herring Pond.

John Doane and the Oakes overshot the mark in going directly to the General Court with their petition to establish a separate township extending to Indian Brook without first making sure that they had the support of the political leaders dwelling south of Billingsgate. In spite of the provisions regarding whaling and oystering, the bill before the Court threatened to exclude the inhabitants of the other parishes not only from the fisheries of Billingsgate Bay and Billingsgate's Herring River, but also from access to the various harbors within Billingsgate Bay – the Herring River, Duck Creek, Blackfish Creek, and Silver Spring Harbor. Furthermore the incorporation of the town of Poole would have seriously reduced Eastham's tax revenues needed to meet expenses additional to those for the two new churches. It is significant that the Eastham town meetings had in preceding years specifically voted the assessment of taxes against the inhabitants of Billingsgate. For instance, in September 1715 the meeting voted "that the Selectmen do forthwith make a rate or assessment on the poles and estates of said town and the district or hamlet of Billingsgate." And again in July 1717 the meeting voted "that the Selectmen ... make a rate or assessment of the poles and estates of the said town in conjunction with the hamlet of Billingsgate as the law directs and according to agreement with said hamlet of the sum of 150 pounds." The voters of Eastham were quite willing that the people of Billingsgate pay for their own schoolmaster and their own minister and build their own meeting house, but they were not ready to forgo Billingsgate's contributions to the town's province tax and other secular expenses or to be shut out of the bountiful resources of

Billingsgate Bay as other towns had been. Here lay the causes of the bitter conflict that was to arise between the two communities.

THE BILLINGSGATE CONSPIRACY

After the defeat of the Billingsgate petition by the June 1718 town meeting, a protracted battle was waged in Boston between John Paine, Eastham's agent, and the influential friends of the Doanes and the Oakes. The strategy adopted by the leaders of the Billingsgate faction was to destroy the credibility of the Eastham town meeting in the eyes of the members of the House by attacking the character of the minister whom the Eastham church had chosen, Samuel Osborn, and thereby to discredit John Paine's arguments against the bill authorizing the secession of Billingsgate. This gambit was to trigger an eruption of dissension that was to beset Billingsgate and Eastham for many years.

It must have seemed, however, an obvious ploy, for the poor Osborn was a vulnerable target. He was, first of all, an Irishman, a product of Trinity College, Dublin, and therefore by origin suspect. He had arrived in Massachusetts in 1707 and had forthwith proceeded to father a bastard child on one Mercy Norton of Martha's Vineyard, for which indiscretion he was convicted by the Court of Common Pleas of Edgartown. He had, it is true, mended his ways by marrying (though not the unhappy Mercy) in 1710 and becoming a schoolmaster in Plymouth, where with the support of Ephraim Little, the minister of that town, he was permitted occasionally to serve as a substitute preacher. Rowland Cotton, the minister in Sandwich, where Osborn had previously taught, recommended the young man as a possibility to the deacons of Eastham, who in November 1717 invited him to preach on a trial basis. The congregation, it was said, was favorably impressed but remained hesitant. On the advice of five ministers Osborn was asked to submit to a formal examination at Sandwich, during which he was required to answer extempore ten questions. Only the sixth, namely, "What is the matter [nature] of a sinner's justification?" did Osborn fail to answer in an acceptable manner. He maintained that the sinner may be freed from the penalty of his sin by good works and that special grace was not therefore the only means of salvation. This rejection of Calvinistic predestination was in effect heretical Arminianism. Nevertheless the ministers gave their overall approval to Osborn's performance, and on May 19, 1718 the assembled members of the church of Eastham extended to him a call. It was nineteen days later, on June 7, that the town meeting rejected John Doane's and Samuel Brown's petition that Billingsgate be permitted to establish itself as a separate town.

There is no evidence that the Doanes or the Oakes had ever heard of Samuel Osborn before 1717, or until June 1718 had given any thought to the question of his fitness for the ministry. Yet all was to be changed by the Eastham town meeting of June 7.

In order to document the case against Osborn and thereby discredit the town of Eastham, Mrs. Doane sailed over to Boston, ostensibly to consult a physician about an ulcerated leg but in fact to gain support from the Boston clergy and obtain a transcript of Osborn's trial at Edgartown. At the same time Oakes and John Doane succeeded in enlisting the Reverend Nathaniel Stone of Harwich as an ally against Osborn. Though Stone had been one of Osborn's examiners at Sandwich and had voted to approve the candidate's dubious performance there, he readily agreed with the Doanes and Oakes that Osborn was wholly unfit to serve as the minister of Eastham or any other place. Indeed Stone became so obsessed by his hostility to Osborn that he was to harass and persecute his unfortunate victim for twenty years and eventually succeed in barring him from every pulpit in New England.

Stone had been the minister of Harwich since 1700. A graduate of Harvard in 1690, he dominated during the fifty-five years of his pastorate the churches of Barnstable County, standing as the champion of predestinarian orthodoxy, of an educated ministry, of strict church discipline, and of the suppression of local church autonomy or heterodoxy. Oakes and the Doanes did not have to work hard to persuade Stone to support them against Osborn, whom he was more than ready to condemn for his lack of Harvard training ("an ignorant stranger, coming out of Ireland without any letters of commendation from sober and religious people there"), a lustful sinner, an Arminian heretic, and a man to whom he felt an instinctive antipathy. Osborn visited him in an attempt to allay his hostility, but to no effect. Stone wrote Rowland Cotton and other ministers during the summer of 1718 to inform them of his opposition to Osborn's ordination. Yet in spite of Stone's efforts the leaders of the Eastham church proceeded with their plans, thereby adding fuel to Stone's indignation.

In order to discredit if not prevent the ordination, Stone drew up a petition against it, of which he gave a copy to Oakes early in September to take from house to house in Billingsgate. Oakes explained to the householders that the purpose of the petition was to assure that a church would be gathered in Billingsgate. This, of course, was true, for the ultimate purpose of the document was to bring about the political and ecclesiastical independence of the hamlet. No copy of the petition has survived, but we may assume that it emphasized Osborn's immoral past, his inveterate ignorance, and his Arminian heterodoxy. It is doubtful that many of those in Billingsgate who were approached understood the nature of this attack on Osborn, for most of those who did sign could not read and some could not even write their own names. In all, Oakes obtained the signatures or marks of seventeen persons, fourteen women and three men, with names such as Swett, Young, Newcomb, Rich, Atkins, Cole, Atwood, and of course Doane.

When on September 17, 1718 Osborn was ordained minister of the new Pochet church, John Doane appeared and presented the petition with its signatures, but he was not able to halt the ceremony. A few days later the deacons commenced an organized effort to induce the signers to recant their opposition. They did succeed in persuading the three men and ten of the women to do so, but four women held out, Esther Atwood, Martha Atkins, Mary Badisha, and Hannah Doane.

In spite of the scandal and the lobbying in Boston by the Doanes and their friends, a majority of the House of Representatives in November refused to concur with the Governor's Council on the bill to create the town of Poole, and the initiative failed.

The following May of 1719 the Reverend Benjamin Webb received a call to be minister of the new "north meeting house" near the Herring Pond in Eastham, and the town voted to build him a dwelling house and pay him £90 a year. Webb appears to have been an innocuous and uncontroversial sort of person; not a word of opposition to his ordination was voiced in Billingsgate.

HANNAH DOANE AND THE DEACONS OF EASTHAM

The issue of Osborn's ordination was, however, by no means dead. A protracted struggle ensued, first between the deacons and the four recalcitrant women, and later between the deacons and Hannah Doane. On June 3, 1719 the church issued an admonition against the four women for "disorderly walking," that is, for having separated themselves from the church and opposed Osborn's ordination. As punishment it barred them from "special ordinances" (the sacraments) "til satisfaction be given." They were summoned to attend at the meeting house on June 16. Esther Atwood, Martha Atkins, and Mary Badisha did appear, accompanied by two of their husbands and Oakes and Stone, but Mrs. Doane wrote that she was unable to appear because of her ulcerated leg, and she asked to be represented by Mr. Stone. The deacons refused, however, to allow Stone to act as advocate for either Mrs. Doane or the other women, and they forced him to withdraw under protest from the meeting house. For several hours the deacons, seconded by one of the husbands, Medad Atwood, pressured the three women until finally they persuaded them to recant and withdraw their opposition to Osborn's ordination.

In October 1719 Mrs. Doane requested dismission from the church, which was granted, but the paper she was given indicated that she was leaving under discipline, and it constituted in effect a dismission for immoral conduct. She firmly refused to accept the document and reportedly made her feelings known in strong and bitter language.

During the summer of 1720 the deacons put other pressures on Mrs. Doane, causing a warrant to be issued against her as a "common disturber of the peace." She was visited at her home by justices of the peace, Mr. Osborn, two of the deacons, and John Paine. She did at length agree to sign a paper asking forgiveness for any offense she might have committed and requesting to be transferred to a Boston church. The Eastham emissaries insisted, however, that she sign a full confession without receiving any guaranties. This she refused to do.

As a consequence on October 22, 1720 the church issued a second admonition against her, this time not for opposing Osborn's ordination but instead for "moral scandal, . . . railing and reviling, . . . contempt of the church's lenity, [and] . . . usurpation of that power and liberty which Christ has denied your sex to speak in church." By these accusations the deacons referred to her intemperate and public refusal to accept the letter of dismission the deacons had tried to force on her the previous October as well as her presumption in defying the will of the deacons. To answer these charges she was summoned to appear at the meeting house on October 31.

Mrs. Doane's response, no doubt advised by Mr. Stone, was to call an ecclesiastical council, as she as an aggrieved member of a church had the right to do, to meet at the Doane house on Chequesset Neck on November 8, 1720. To this council she invited, in addition to delegates from Eastham, the Reverend Nathaniel Stone and Deacon Lincoln of Harwich; the Reverend Joseph Lord, recently ordained, and Deacon Thomas Atkins of Chatham; and the Reverend John Avery of Truro. Also invited but not attending were the Reverend Daniel Greenleaf of Yarmouth and the Reverend Jonathan Russell of Barnstable as well as deacons from these two towns.

The council considered only the first admonition, the charge of "disorderly walking," and the question of the right of the church to bar Mrs. Doane from the sacraments for refusing to accept Mr. Osborn's ordination. Predictably the verdict was to exonerate her first on grounds of freedom of conscience and, second, by reason of Mr. Osborn's "blemishes," namely, his having fathered a bastard child, borne false witness against Mercy Norton, the child's mother, and falsified the facts regarding the whole episode. Mrs. Doane, the council decided, should suffer no blame for her failure to attend "public ordinances," for she had been prevented by bodily indisposition. The entire admonition was rejected as "male administration" (maladministration). Mrs. Doane, freed from censure, should be given, the council concluded, an unqualified dismission from the church in Eastham, and the members of the church should put on a sense of sin and error and avoid all exasperating reflections.[11]

In response the church at Eastham called a meeting at Yarmouth attended by the ministers Rowland Cotton of Sandwich, Daniel Greenleaf of Yarmouth, Jonathan Russell of Barnstable, Nathaniel Stone of Harwich, and Joseph Lord of Chatham. They sustained the verdict of the Billingsgate Council by recommending, on the one hand, that the church at Eastham should "signify a sense of error" for having admonished and debarred Hannah Doane for refusing to accept Mr. Osborn (the first admonition) and, on the other, that if she were indeed guilty of other "moral scandals" (the second admonition) the church members should forbear giving her a dismission until "they have proceeded with her according to gospel rule."

Mrs. Doane triumphantly wrote the deacons at Eastham that if they would confess in writing their sin and error in committing "male administration" and give her a written proof of their allegations she would gladly acknowledge her faults, if any she had, in writing. The deacons made no reply.

Instead on December 4, 1720 the church issued a third admonition, attempting to shift the issue from Osborn's qualifications (or lack thereof) to Hannah Doane's moral character. The deacons now refused to grant her a dismission, reiterated the accusation of "immoral practices," and charged that she had "greatly increased and aggravated [her] guilt" and "discovered much deceit" in summoning the Billingsgate Council. They "rejected" her for "railleries and ungodly conversation."

Finally in 1721 the church in Eastham solemnly excommunicated Mrs. Doane. In retaliation, the ministers Lord, Stone, and Avery excommunicated the entire membership of the church in Eastham.

'This was still far from the end of the dispute. In the autumn of 1721 the Eastham deacons circulated a document known as the "Potchy Paper," justifying their past actions and announcing a plan to call an ecclesiastical council in Eastham in October of 1722 to rule on whether the Billingsgate Council had been a "regular" council and its acts just. Stone, Avery, and Lord, refusing to attend, in justification wrote and published in Boston a fifty-six-page work entitled *The Result of a Council Held at Billingsgate . . . With Illustration of the Reasons against Joining with Eastham in Calling a Council.*

Possibly because of their opposition, the Eastham Council was delayed. It met on October 24, 1722 but immediately was adjourned for lack of delegates. Nevertheless it was reconvened successfully on May 8, 1723, this time attended by ministers from eleven churches, four in Barnstable County, three in Plymouth County, and four elsewhere in Massachusetts, together with eight lay messengers including two provincial councillors and five judges. Stone, Avery, and Lord once more refused to attend as delegates, but both Stone and representatives of the church at Eastham presented briefs, and Hannah Doane, John Doane, and Josiah Oakes all testified.

The delegates appear to have made a valiant effort to achieve a tenable compromise and to bring peace to the dissension-riven churches of Barnstable County. They refused to rule on whether the Billingsgate Council was regular or not, one of the two issues they had been convened to settle. The ministers Lord, Avery, and Stone might well have been justified, the council advised, in removing the first admonition, which had denied the four women the right to reject a minister they considered unworthy to be ordained. Hannah Doane had raised two important issues, freedom of conscience and the role of women in church government. On these essential questions she appears to have been sustained by the Eastham Council of 1723. It signified little that the delegates thought that the Billingsgate Council should not have gone so far as to accuse the church in Eastham of "male administration" or that Mrs. Doane did deserve the second admonition for her "railings." The fundamental decision was that she and her neighbors had the right to oppose Osborn's ordination. Moreover in their effort to bring peace the delegates advised that the too hasty excommunication of Mrs. Doane should be withdrawn and that she should be allowed to confess her errors and receive a dismission from the church. The Council censured the publication of *The Result of the Council* as tending "to stir up strife" and it also urged the leaders of the church at Eastham not to publish a reply.

THE VINDICATION OF THE RIGHT TO POLITICAL AND ECCLESIASTICAL AUTONOMY

Despite these earnest attempts at conciliation, it was impossible to ignore the fact that the Eastham Council of 1723 did uphold the right of the individual (or of a group of individuals, such as the hamlet of Billingsgate) to reject the authority of an established church. It is by no means certain that this principle was the one that either the Doanes or Josiah Oakes or Nathaniel Stone intended to champion, but it was the principle that did in fact prevail.

This point was shortly to be made clear by the General Court. At a town meeting held on August 2, 1721, at the very time that Hannah Doane was being excommunicated, two questions had been put to the inhabitants of Eastham: first, "whether the town are willing to take in Billingsgate Society, so as to make three precincts or societies and maintain the ministers in equal proportion"; or second, "whether the town were willing to set off Billingsgate society to be a precinct to extend southerly as far as Indian Brook." Both questions "passed in the negative," that is, were defeated.
The vote was inevitable in the midst of the Hannah Doane controversy, but the town's position was now ultimately untenable. The people of Billingsgate had already achieved what the people of Eastham were

trying to deny to them. Josiah Oakes had been preaching regularly to the inhabitants of Billingsgate in the little meeting house on Chequesset Neck for nearly three years when on March 14, 1721 a number of the inhabitants met together, no doubt at the instigation of the Doanes, in order to name Oakes as their minister. The document they drew up recorded a vote by the "Inhabitants of the Hamlet of Billingsgate." "Having for several years," they wrote, "with good agreement supported the Gospel ministry among us [and] ... having met ... to consider the most proper method for ... the founding of a Church of Christ in this place, ... [we] have made choice of the Rev. Mr. Josiah Oakes to dispense the word and ordinances to or among us." A settlement was promised to Mr. Oakes: "Four acres of land ... and to fence the same ... and that he shall have the improvements [use and benefits] of the ministerial lands and meddows in said hamlet [as voted by the Eastham town meeting in 1711] for fencing, firing, planting, and herbage." His salary from "the second day of June next ensuing June 2, 1721] till the second day of June of the following year, which will be 1722, [shall] be sixty pounds and board as formerly, from thence forward so long as he should continue to be a minister to be eighty pound current money annually." Since Mr. Webb in Eastham had been offered a salary of 90 pounds a year in 1719, the terms of Oakes' contract were not overly generous.

This unsigned document probably had no legal force, for the authors (whoever they were) had no standing as members or officers of a town meeting or a precinct or parish meeting, and they had no power to raise or appropriate money for any purpose or to dispose of land designated by the Eastham town meeting for ministerial use. Nevertheless about two and a half months before the Eastham town meeting refused to acknowledge the existence of a parish, precinct, or church in Billingsgate these people had of their own claimed inherent power and in defiance of a legally established town and church constituted themselves an ecclesiastical and political entity.

A year later certain persons, presumably inhabitants of Billingsgate, once again met and endorsed the original document: "March 12, 1722, voted and a Clear vote it was for the above written proposal to be as written above." The need now was to give legal sanction to this asserted political autonomy.

This time John Doane did not waste time presenting a petition to the Eastham town meeting but instead submitted one to the General Court on June 16, 1722 jointly with "Israel Bacon" (Isaac Baker) as "Agents for the Hamlet of Billingate [sic] in the Township of Eastham, &c., praying that they may be made a Lawful Precinct from Truro-Line to Indian-brook." The petitioners were granted liberty to bring in a bill, and in November John Cushing, John Dyer, and Israel Tupper of the House of Representatives were appointed a committee to repair to Billingsgate and Eastham, investigate the situation, and report back to the Court, which they did on May 14, 1723, eleven months later.

Meanwhile the Eastham town meeting, having received a copy of Billingsgate's petition to the General Court, appointed John Paine once more to act as the town's agent before the Court, and it also named Samuel Knowles and Isaac Pepper to serve with Paine as a committee to wait upon the committee named by the House of Representatives. As far as the record shows, these were the only actions taken by Eastham in response to Billingsgate's initiative. No new vote was taken on the previously refused petition of 1721 and no resolution was debated or voted in respect to the bill before the General Court. It was as though the town meeting's negative vote of August 2, 1721 had never been taken. Hannah Doane's rejection of the authority of the church at Eastham had been swallowed up in the rejection of the town of Eastham by the community of Billingsgate, a rejection about to be sanctioned by the General Court.

Upon receipt on May 14, 1723 of the committee's thorough and conscientious report, the House carefully examined and debated the problems presented. Acting on the committee's recommendations, the General Court amended the original bill so as to permit four families dwelling on the southern limits of Billingsgate who had not petitioned to be set off to the parish of Billingsgate to remain with their estates in the old north parish of Eastham so long as they desired. The inhabitants of Billingsgate otherwise were granted all the powers and privileges enjoyed by precincts, were authorized to procure and settle an orthodox minister, and were exempted from any charges for the maintenance of the ministry in other or southward parts of Eastham. John Doane, Esq., "Principal Inhabitant of the said precinct," was directed to notify and summon the inhabitants duly qualified as voters to meet and choose precinct officers and determine the way and method for future meetings.

As instructed, John Doane ordered the inhabitants of Billingsgate to assemble on June 24, 1723 in the Chequesset Neck meeting house, where they elected him, Isaac Baker, and Ebenezer Freeman as "selectmen or assessors" and John Rich as clerk and treasurer and "voted Mr. Oks continue our proper minister for the time that was proposed for until the last of July next ensuing." At the second precinct meeting held on July 29 it was voted "that the Revd. Josiah Oakes shall continue in the work of the ministry as formerly in the precinct for the salary of 80 pound a year."

Thus all the issues seemed resolved. Yet this was far from true.

Just when Oakes' salary of £80 was being confirmed, Nathaniel Stone and Joseph Lord, notwithstanding the prudent advice of the Eastham Council, prolonged the dispute between Samuel Osborn and Hannah Doane by publishing in Boston a second polemic entitled *The Veracity and Equity of the Members of the Council Held at Billingsgate* in *Eastham, 1720, Asserted and Maintained.* To this Osborn replied in the following year, 1724, with *A Church of Christ Vindicated. A Short and Plain Relation of Some Transactions in the South Church at Eastham Forced into the Publick by Several Sallacious Pamphlets That Have Been Lately Published.* Stone and Lord continued their attacks on Osborn with further publications in 1725, 1728, 1732, and 1735. The eventual consequence was a second Eastham Council in 1738 to examine formally the continuously repeated charges against Osborn of various doctrinal errors, principally the old accusation of Arminianism and belief in salvation by good works. Stone finally triumphed, for the Council first suspended and then removed Osborn from the church at

Pochet. In 1743 the unhappy man published in Boston his final defense and an account of his tribulations in *The Case and Complaint of Mr. Samuel Osborn Late of Eastham.*

The feud between Stone and Osborn and the theological doctrines and ecclesiastical principles which were the ostensible subjects of their polemic had long since ceased to be of immediate concern to the inhabitants of Billingsgate. Mrs. Doane's battle against the deacons of Eastham had been political, not doctrinal, and with the support of the General Court she had won. By the time the Reverend Mr. Stone drove the unfortunate Mr. Osborn from his pulpit in Pochet, Mrs. Doane was dead, Josiah Oakes was dead, John Doane had shaken the sand of Billingsgate from his feet, and the people of the north precinct had been forced to confront a new but equally difficult political crisis.

Chapter III

THE ORDEAL OF JOSIAH OAKES

When in June 1722 John Doane and Isaac Baker presented to the General Court their petition that Billingsgate be made a separate precinct the hamlet was united (with the exceptions of the four families in Hither Billingsgate dwelling just north of Indian Brook) in supporting this demand for autonomy. The Court was to free the inhabitants from the long and arduous trip to the Eastham meetinghouse, relieve them of the taxes they had been paying to the town of Eastham, and give them the management of their own local affairs, ecclesiastical and secular. They were also united, to all appearances, in accepting Josiah Oakes, who had been preaching to them for eight years and had buried his father in the new burying ground on Chequesset Neck. If there were those who favored him less than others did, they forbore voicing their reservations publicly. But seeds of dissension had been sown.

THE COMING OF MARGARET HOUGH

Sometime in 1721 or 1722 Hannah Doane's young cousin Margaret Hough sailed over from Boston to live with the Doanes, with whom, the reader will recall, Josiah Oakes had been living for eight years. Margaret Hough was the great-great-granddaughter of Atherton Hough, who had accompanied John Cotton to New England in 1633. By a curious coincidence her younger brother, Atherton, also to be a guest of the Doanes in Billingsgate, years later was to marry John Doane's widow and third wife, Jane Baxter, whom Doane was to marry after Hannah's death in 1731. Margaret Hough was born March 10, 1701, so she was a young woman of twenty or twenty-one when she came ashore on

Chequesset Neck in 1721 or 1722 to bring to Josiah Oakes, who was himself only thirty-three, the conditions of his tragedy.

During the year 1722 while living with the Doanes Margaret gave birth to a child. Preserved in the Archives of the Commonwealth are two lengthy affidavits recounting in considerable circumstantial detail this untoward event. One was dictated by a woman named Mary Ireland, the wife of a tenant and servant of the Doanes living in a small house near the Doanes, and the other was an account by the widow Mary Swett, who dwelt near where the King's Highway crossed Herring Brook. In neither narrative, nor in any other document relating to the episode, is there any hint that Margaret Hough could have become pregnant after arriving in Billingsgate or that Josiah Oakes, with whom she was sharing the Doanes' hospitality, could have been responsible. We must therefore infer that the dates of her arrival and of the birth made clear that she had arrived already pregnant. It seems most likely that her unfortunate condition was the result of an indiscretion committed elsewhere and that her family, anxious to conceal or minimize the scandal, had prevailed on cousin Hannah to provide a refuge for their errant daughter. In a graphic account Mary Ireland told how she had prepared a cradle for the baby in the rear of her one-room cottage and how at the last moment she had been told by Sam, the Doanes' Negro slave, that other arrangements had been made. What these were we do not know, for the baby was taken away, leaving no trace of its fate.

It will be recalled that a year later on July 29, 1723 the second precinct meeting voted apparently without dissent to continue Mr. Oakes in the ministry. Yet by the following spring there were expressions of opposition to the young minister. The meeting of March 31, 1724 elected John Doane as moderator and reelected him, Isaac Baker, and Ebenezer Freeman as selectmen or assessors. The only other business placed before the meeting was to enter in the precinct records Oakes' formal acceptance of the call voted on July 29, 1723 and also his acceptance of the original unofficial call of March 14, 1721. Yet it was apparent that a minority of those present were strongly opposed to Oakes' continuing, and on April 15 this group drew up a petition to that effect. "We are very tender," they wrote ambiguously, "concerning Mr. Oaks and would not disclose our reasons any faster or further than necessity required, and with good advice at a time convenient are ready to give reasons." This document was signed by twenty men, including Ebenezer Freeman (the selectman-assessor), Daniel Mayo, Samuel Smith, George Williamson, Barnabas Young, and Israel Young. These were men of substance and influence in the precinct.

We are obliged to speculate about the grounds for these reservations, but it seems obvious that many in Billingsgate must have objected to the relations between Josiah Oakes and Margaret Hough. Since Oakes had been preaching in Billingsgate for ten years, any new feeling against him must have arisen from recent developments. What had developed could have been only tender feelings shared by this young unmarried couple dwelling intimately in the same house. Margaret's earlier demonstration of what might be called her pregnability may have stimulated mutual affection; it seems even more likely that it stimulated the neighbors to suspect the existence of such sentiments. In any case, their reality was later proved by the couple's marriage on November 10, 1724. That the young pair had been impatient to enjoy connubial pleasures was also suggested by the birth of their daughter Hannah on May 16, 1725, a bit more than six months after the wedding.

It must not be supposed that fornication was unknown, or rare, in Barnstable County in the early eighteenth century, even among the religiously minded. In addition to the example of Samuel Osborn there was the case of the Reverend Mr. Fessenden of Sandwich, who after repeated questioning by his parishioners finally confessed to premarital relations with his betrothed. In 1725 the tolerant Reverend Mr. Ebenezer Gay preached in Barnstable on the text "Ministers are men of like passions with others." Even Nathaniel Stone was willing to baptize children born too soon and welcome their parents back into the church, though only after they had publicly confessed their sin. In a community the size of Billingsgate, which in 1724 contained about three hundred souls, there could have been few secrets, and the dalliance attributed to the young minister and the notorious Margaret Hough (her frailty all too manifest) must have been the subject of endless gossip. If Josiah Oakes had been a strong and esteemed figure it is possible that his parishioners might have been more indulgent. One has, however, the unverified impression that he was a person of weak and vacillating will, dominated by the strong-minded Doanes and not widely liked though at first tolerated and treated with respect because of his powerful patrons. When he fell from grace he did not find ready forgiveness. There was also the fact, as events were to make evident, that so wealthy, powerful, and domineering a couple as the Doanes aroused a measure of resentment, a resentment that found convenient expression against their erring protege. Indeed, the Doanes' unhesitating support of Oakes was an indication that they clearly saw that their own political power in the precinct was at risk.

THE RISE OF THE ANTI-OAKES PARTY

In any event, the opposition to Mr. Oakes increased. The June 1, 1724 precinct meeting was adjourned by John Doane as moderator, probably to give himself and Oakes time to rally their supporters, and was reconvened on June 22. The plan conceived by the Oakes faction was to induce the precinct meeting to reconfirm the settlement initially granted in 1721, but with important changes. In addition to the £80 annual salary and the four acres of upland previously promised, he was now to receive a cash settlement of £120, one half at the end of 1724 and the other half at the end of 1725, to which he was to have, however, permanent title only if he built or bought a house in Billingsgate and remained in the ministry there for twenty years or life.

Intense political maneuvering took place before the June 22 meeting. William Covel later testified in an affidavit that Mr. Oakes invited him and others to meet at the Doanes' house the morning before the meeting in a caucus to firm up the support of the Doane party. Joseph Lord reported that John Rich, the precinct clerk, was heard to say that the motion to appoint Mr. Oakes for twenty years was made because his supporters feared that if the vote were to appoint him for only one year it would never again be possible to muster a majority to reappoint him for any period of time.

Sixty votes were cast at the meeting, thirty in favor of the proposed settlement, twenty-eight opposed, and two "neuters." Eight qualified voters were either absent or failed to have their votes recorded, if we may trust the assessors' list of 1724. It is a curious fact that no record has survived of the names of those who voted in the affirmative. The two "neuters" were Joseph Atkins and Charles Paine. Voting against the proposed settlement were Samuel Brown, Thomas Brown, James Cahoon, Elisha Cole, William Cole, Ebenezer Eldrige [Eldridge], Elisha Eldrige senior, Elisha Eldrige junior, Ebenezer Freeman, Eleazer Hamlin [Hamblin], Elisha Hamlin, Benjamin Hamlin, Daniel Mayo, Elisha Mayo, Jeremiah Mayo, Samuel Mayo, Bryant Morton, Samuel Smith, Benjamin Sweat [Swett or Sweet], John Treat, Nathaniel Treat, Moses Wile, George Williamson, Barnabas Young, Benjamin Young, Israel Young, John Young, and Jonathan Young.

Since not all the eligible inhabitants voted, it is impossible to reconstruct with certainty the list of affirmative voters. We may, however, be sure that it included Isaac Baker, the selectman-assessor; Isaac Doane, John's brother; John Doane; and John Ireland, John Doane's tenant. Probable are Richard Arey, Joseph Atkins, Thomas Atkins, John Atwood, William Badisha, Isaac Doane junior, Thomas Gross, Abiah Harding, Thomas Newcomb senior, Thomas Newcomb junior, and John Rich.

On August 11, 1724 the opponents of Oakes issued a lengthy statement contesting the validity of the vote of June 22. The forty-three who signed the protest included all but two of those who had voted in the negative on June 22 and in addition seventeen who presumably had been absent on June 22 or else had voted for the settlement or been "neuters" and had changed sides: Joseph Atkins junior, Eleazer Atwood, Medad Atwood, Samuel Atwood, William Brown, David Cole, Nathaniel Covel, William Covel senior, John Hallet, William Lewis, Simon Newcomb junior, Charles Paine, Isaac [Pearce(?)], Robert Rich, Solomon Sweat [Swett], George Ward, and Daniel Young.

The signers claimed that more than twenty-eight negative voters had been present on June 22, some of whom had not been counted, and that at least one of the thirty affirmative votes had not been valid. They also made the point that in issuing the call to Mr. Oakes the precinct had not sought the advice of three neighboring ministers as was required by law. They could also have pointed out that Oakes had never been ordained.

More fuel was added to the fire in November 1724 when the Reverend Nathaniel Stone came to Billingsgate to marry Josiah Oakes and Margaret Hough, by this time three months pregnant.

THE ASSESSORS' LIST OF NOVEMBER 1724

According to the provisions of the vote of June 22, 1724, £60, one half of the settlement of £120, were due Mr. Oakes by December 31, 1724. In addition he had been promised £60 salary for the fiscal year 1721-1722 (June 2 to June 2) and £80 a year commencing June 2, 1722. Since Oakes was to sue in July 1725 for the £80 due on June 2, 1725, we may assume that he had been paid for the fiscal year 1721-22 £60 and a total of £160 for the two fiscal years 1722-23 and 1723-24. Inasmuch as no precinct taxes were assessed until November 1724, it is probable that these salaries through June 2, 1724 were paid from voluntary contributions by the Doanes and others. Nothing had yet been paid on the promised £120 settlement.*

Now, however, half of the £120 settlement would be due December 31, 1724 and £80 of salary would be payable the following June. These were by law the responsibility of the precinct. Consequently the assessors, acting in compliance with the vote of the precinct meeting of July 29,

*Oakes in a petition dated July 6, 1725 to the Court of General Sessions in Barnstable wrote: 'They [the precinct] have not set out his [Oakes') 4 acres of Land aforesaid nor paid him the sd £120 or any part of it nor the yearly salary of £80 due June 2d 1725 or any part of it." Suffolk County Court Records, Case No. 19536(3).

1723, drew up an assessors' list of taxes on the poles and real and personal properties of the inhabitants and property owners of the precinct. This document, preserved in the records of the Suffolk County Court, provides interesting information. Of the ninety-six names listed, twenty-eight were of persons who were not assessed either pole taxes or personal property taxes, that is, who owned real property within the precinct but resided elsewhere. This left a total of sixty-eight taxpaying residents and heads of households, including the widow Mary Swett.

In spite of the fact that before 1694 grants of upland and dwelling lots in Billingsgate had been made only to the heads of the fourteen families of Purchasers or their assigns, by 1724 most of these grants had been sold to newcomers. Only the Doanes, the Coles, and the Freemans still held significant real property in Billingsgate. John Doane's real estate was taxed at £1 8s.; his brother Isaac's at 4s. 2d.; that of his brother David, a physician who lived in Eastham, at ls. 4d.; and that of his cousin Thomas, a blacksmith who had moved to Chatham, at 2s. 8d. As for the Coles, William's real estate was taxed at 3s., Elisha's at 3s. 4d., and Eleazer's at 3s. Ebenezer Freeman's more considerable holding beside Herring Brook was taxed at 5s. 2d. Among the nonresident property owners there were Edward and Joshua Bangs, heirs of the Purchaser Edward Bangs, with holdings taxed at 2s. and 4 s.; Joseph and another Higgins, descendants of Richard Higgins, with property taxed at 2s. and ls.; John Mulford, the brother of Thomas senior, taxed at ls. 4d.; and Thomas Mulford, presumably the son of Thomas Mulford senior, taxed at 2s.

The large majority of the taxpayers were members of families that had arrived in Billingsgate and Eastham soon after the first settlements. The Mayos, Daniel, Samuel, and Elisha; were descendants of Eastham's first minister, John Mayo, who was pastor from 1646 to 1655. The two Joseph Atkins, senior and junior, were presumably the son and grandson of Henry Atkins, who owned a Billingsgate meadow in 1659. Samuel, Thomas, and William Brown were probably the sons of the William Brown who bought land near Silver Spring in 1672. The Atwoods, Eleazer, Medad, Samuel, Eldad, Benjamin, Joshua, and John, were descendants of Stephen Atwood, 1620-1694, who received a grant of fifty acres in Eastham in 1672.

More recent settlers were the Eldridges. Elisha Eldridge senior received a grant at the head of Duck Creek as late as 1709; Elisha junior and Ebenezer were no doubt his sons. John Swett, the former husband of the widow Mary Swett and probably the father of Benjamin Swett, had been a squatter who, we know, received title to the land under his dwelling in 1700. Others must have been more recent arrivals and some have left no trace. Of Abraham Lyon, for instance, we know nothing except that his name appeared on this assessors' list of 1724.

The assessments indicate a wide variation in the wealth of individuals and the existence of a large number of inhabitants of meager means. Fifteen resident taxpayers (22%) of the sixty-eight residents possessed no real property. Some of these, such as Isaac Doane junior, were probably living on their fathers' properties, but most seem to have been landless tenants or servants. These included John Ireland and probably also James Cahoon, John Hallet, Abraham Lyon, Bryant Morton, Edward Newcomb, and Charles Paine. Fourteen men (21%) paid the minimum real estate tax of eight pence, which may be contrasted with the maximum tax of 336d. (£1 8s.), the average of30d. (2s. 6d.), and the mean of 16d. (1s. 4d.). The personal property taxes extended over a similar wide range. Twenty-six persons paid 44d. (3s. 8d.) or less, a figure to be contrasted with the maximum of 464d. (£1 18s. 8d.), an average of 92d. (7s. 8d.), a median of 68d. (5s. 8d.), and a minimum of 28d. (2s. 4d.). The combined real and personal property taxes ranged from a maximum of 800d. (£3 6s. 8d.) to a minimum of 28d. (2s. 4d.). The average was 120d. (10s.) and the median 96d. (8s.). Those in the lowest quartile paid 48d. (4s.) or less. Close to one half of the resident taxpayers (29 or 43%) owned no real estate or were taxed at the minimum rate of 8d. for real property. There was a high correlation between real and personal property taxes.

All these data indicate the existence of an impoverished group of about twenty-four male heads of households plus the widow Mary Swett, comprising 37% of the resident taxpayers and paying combined personal and property taxes of 52d. or lower. Above these on the lowest economic level, the combined tax assessments were distributed very evenly up the scale from 60d. (5s.) to 264d. (£1 2s.). Heading the upper middle group was Samuel Smith with a combined tax of 448d. (£1 17s. 4d.), of which £1 14s. was the tax on his stock and furnishings as a merchant or tavern keeper, but far higher still was the combined tax of John Doane, £3 6s. 8d.

The grand total of the combined pole, real, and personal property taxes which could be raised on the assessments of November 1724 was £60 4s. 5d., a sum that fell far short of the £140 needed: £80 for Oakes' salary due June 2, 1725 and the first £60 installment on his settlement, due December 31, 1724.

These fiscal details and the economic stratification in Billingsgate that they reveal had political and social significance. It seems likely that part of the opposition to Josiah Oakes was caused by the perception that he was an expense the bottom third of the population of the precinct could ill afford. It would be misleading, however, to give too much weight to the economic motive, for among Oakes' opponents were some of the wealthier men in the precinct such as Samuel Brown, Daniel Mayo, Barnabas Young, Benjamin Young, Israel Young, and especially Samuel Smith. It is more likely that John Doane's great wealth coupled with his and Hannah's arrogance and overweening presumption were what alienated both the poor and those of moderate or comfortable means. The language of the affidavits dictated or written by various men and women of Billingsgate reveals clearly that while Josiah Oakes' behavior with Margaret Hough lost him the respect of the people, their enmity and exasperation were directly mainly against John and Hannah Doane. The very considerable influence Squire Doane had exerted over the community until 1723 melted like snow in a February thaw. The revolution was not religious or moralistic but political and social.

THE ANTI-OAKES PARTY TAKES CONTROL

At the February 26, 1725 precinct meeting the anti-Oakes faction took control by electing Jonathan Young as moderator in place of John Doane, but no other significant action was taken. The warrant for the following meeting to elect officers and to raise and appropriate money for Oakes' salary and settlement was signed by John Doane, Isaac Baker, and two who remained loyal to the Doanes, John Atwood and Thomas Gross, but it was to be of no effect. The meeting, held on March 29, elected an entirely anti-Oakes slate of officers: Samuel Brown as moderator; Jonathan Young as clerk; Samuel Smith as treasurer; Elisha Eldridge, Samuel Smith, and Jonathan Young as assessors; and Elisha Eldridge, Eleazer Hamblin, Samuel Smith, George Williamson, and Jonathan Young as a committee to warn (summon) the next meeting and unofficially to act as a sort of precinct directorate. Every one of these men had voted against Oakes' settlement on June 22, 1724. They drew up a new warrant for an April meeting "to reasume the vote that was supposed to be past on June 22, 1724 relating to Mr. Josiah Oakes continuing in the work of the ministry" and setting his salary; and also in order "to choose some person or persons as agents ... to forbid Mr. Oakes any more preaching in the meeting house, ... to advize with our neighboring ministers, ... to look out for a minister, [and] ... to agree upon what sum of money to raise this year for the support of the ministry."

The meeting was duly held on April 19, 1725 under the guidance of the new moderator, and it "voted ... that those votes that was [sic] supposed to be passed on June 22, 1724 above said Relating to Mr. Josiah Oakes continuing in the work of the ministry among us twenty years or during life as also those votes relating to the assessors Raising said Oakes Salary and Settlement shall be void and of no Effect." Elisha Eldridge junior and George Williamson were elected agents to forbid Oakes' preaching in the meeting house and Samuel Brown and Samuel Smith agents to advise with the neighboring ministry. The meeting voted to raise £90 for the support of the ministry.

A month later, on May 16, Margaret Oakes gave birth to a baby girl. The Oakes claimed that the child was born prematurely but no one believed them. Sarah Covel, the wife of William, later testified: "Mrs. Doane signifyed as if it was a poor little creature and bornd before the time. I told her it was really my opinion that it was as large and thriving a child as some that was borned amongst us near about that time that I named to her, that we had no reason to think were brned before their time." It was at this juncture that the anti-Oakes party persuaded the widow Mary Swett to dictate her affidavit testifying to the circumstances of Margaret Hough's first pregnancy in 1722.

On July 6, 1725 Oakes with Doane's support filed a petition with the Court of General Sessions in Barnstable to require the precinct to pay him £80 as his annual salary for the fiscal year 1724-1725, as had been voted on July 29, 1723 and as had been due on June 2, 1725. This suit was supported by another petition signed by John Doane and fifteen others and also by an affidavit signed by Nathaniel Stone and Joseph Lord denouncing as "vile fabrications" the allegations that Oakes had been guilty of fornication and other scandalous works. The case dragged on from July to October 1725; Oakes' recorded "Bill of Costs" shows that he attended the court frequently. The decision finally rendered in October was against Oakes, but he appealed to the Superior Court in Plymouth, which on April 26, 1726 reversed the verdict of the court in Barnstable and awarded Oakes £80 for services rendered to the precinct from June 2, 1724 to June 2, 1725, plus costs.

The essential question was whether the precinct had the power to dismiss a minister who had received and accepted a call from the congregation. Moreover, even if the precinct meeting was empowered to dismiss him, it had no authority to bar him from preaching in the meeting house, which was the property not of the precinct but of John Doane, Isaac Baker, Israel Young, and the other proprietors of the building.

In an effort to reach an agreement with Oakes the precinct meeting of June 14, 1726 appointed a committee composed of Samuel Brown,

Eleazer Hamblin, John Rich, Samuel Smith, and Jonathan Young, all except John Rich being anti-Oakes men. A couple of weeks later John Atwood and Isaac Baker, both of the Oakes faction, were added, presumably in the hope that their presence would make the committee more acceptable to Oakes and Doane. It soon became apparent, however, that no negotiated compromise was possible, so on July 11 another precinct meeting was held, which voted to call an ecclesiastical council. To this Oakes agreed. He nevertheless presented in October 1726 another petition to the Court of General Sessions in Barnstable for his salary for the fiscal year 1725-1726.

THE SECOND BILLINGSGATE COUNCIL, 1726-1727

On November 2, 1726 the second Billingsgate Council met, composed of six ministers: John Avery of Truro, Nathaniel Eells of Scituate, Joseph Green of Barnstable East, Daniel Lewis of Pembroke, Timothy Ruggles of Rochester, and Samuel Spear of Provincetown. Benjamin Colman of Boston, the Reverend Mr. Webb of Boston, and William Williams of Weston declined.

After a number of sessions the council adjourned for the winter to meet again in the spring of 1727. Meanwhile the Court of General Sessions had again denied Doane's petition for his annual salary, and once more he had appealed to the Superior Court in Plymouth, and again the Barnstable decision had been reversed and Oakes had been awarded £80 for his services from June 2, 1725 to June 2, 1726, plus costs.

On May 3, 1727 the Ecclesiastical Council at Billingsgate reconvened with the same delegates except for the absence of Samuel Spear of Provincetown. Predictably the council sought a tenable middle ground. Its judgment was that Oakes' solicitation of signatures for the petition that Stone had composed against Mr. Osborn in 1718 was "not performed with that simplicity which became Him," and that he had been rash and imprudent in saying that he and Mr. Doane "would wholly break up this place unless it would settle him to be their minister." On the other hand they found no evidence of fornication or of four other allegations against Mr. Oakes. They advised the people to have due regard for the opinion of Mr. Doane and they professed to believe that Mr. Oakes was qualified for the ministry elsewhere. They found, however, in the precinct "universal dislike of him and dissent from him." Seventy-four of the inhabitants, forty-four males, of whom thirty-eight were heads of families, and thirty females, all married, had signed a statement of dissent. The council also pointed out that all eight formally professed male members of the church resident in Billingsgate had refused Mr. Oakes, and also that he had never been ordained. Under these conditions, the council concluded, there was no prospect of Mr. Oakes' exercising the ministry in Billingsgate, and they advised mutual forgiveness and the payment to Mr. Oakes of the money due him.

Nathaniel Stone, like Joseph Lord, had not been invited to participate in the council. He wrote a strong letter to the delegates protesting that they had not been a legitimate ecclesiastical council, for the precinct was not an ecclesiastical society qualified to call such a council and Mr. Oakes was "not a settled ordained minister," and therefore any complaints should have been addressed to Oakes' own church in Boston. In any case, said Stone somewhat disingenuously, Oakes was being condemned "only for swerving from the Gospel rule in conversation."

Following the council, a precinct meeting voted to close the meeting house to Oakes, who had continued up to this point to preach there. This prohibition occasioned a sharp letter from Nathaniel Eells, one of the delegates to the council, who felt strongly that the precinct should not have excluded Oakes from the pulpit until another minister had been called.

The difficult problem was the physical removal of Oakes from the meeting house. At this stage of the episode, John Doane seems to have assumed an ambiguous position. He apparently did not explicitly oppose the recommendations made by the ecclesiastical council and he consented to serve on a committee with George Williamson and John Rich to seek the help and advice of the president and fellows of Harvard

College in finding a new minister, On the other hand, as we shall see, he supported Oakes in his refusal to vacate the meeting house.

THE ORDEAL OF JOHN SUMNER

On Saturday, June 24, 1727, John Sumner, a candidate recommended by Harvard, arrived in Billingsgate to preach to the people of the precinct. The next day being Sunday, it was decided that he should hold his first service not in the meeting house but in a private dwelling in order to avoid a confrontation with Oakes. The following Sunday, July 2, the committee "was disappointed by Mr. Oakes being got into the meeting house very early in the morning whereupon we were forced to return to a private house." The third Sunday, July 9, John Rich later recounted, "I came to the meeting house about seven o'clock in the morning and there were Mr. Doane walking about the house and Mr. Oakes in the pulpit, and two young men were in the house, namely Atherton Hough [Margaret Oakes' younger brother] and one Whealdon." Oakes and Doane refused to leave the meeting house, "whereupon we were forst to a private house again."

For the fourth Sunday, July 16, the committee made elaborate preparations to forestall the occupation of the meeting house by the Oakes faction. Concerning the events of that dramatic and memorable morning we have in the Archives of the Commonwealth affidavits by [H——?] Bosworth, Elisha Eldridge, Jiddian Ellis, Ebenezer Freeman, Benjamin Hamblin, Eleazer Hamblin, Thomas Newcomb, Jane Perce, John Rich, Mary Sagan, and Israel Young. From their accounts we may picture many details of the interior of the meeting house and of the incidents that occurred there.

As one entered the door at the west end one faced a narrow "alley," on each side of which were pews, partitioned spaces in which chairs or benches were placed, each pew being provided with a hinged door opening out into the alley. The front pew on the right belonged to the Doanes; that on the left was reserved for the deacons. At the far end of the alley against the east wall was the raised pulpit, to which the minister ascended by stairs and entered through a door. On either side of the pulpit were probably more chairs or benches.

Before seven o'clock in the morning of the sixteenth Eleazer Atwood and Israel Young had stationed themselves in the pulpit and Benjamin Hamblin had taken a position on the pulpit stairs. Daniel and Jeremiah Mayo were in the deacons' pew to the left of the pulpit. At seven o'clock John Doane, Josiah Oakes, their wives, and others of the Doane family filed in and entered the Doane pew on the right. Under John Doane's prompting, Oakes ascended the pulpit stairs and placed a hand on the pulpit door, but Israel Young, standing in the pulpit, told him to forbear, and he turned back. There was next an exchange of sharp words between John Doane and Eleazer Atwood, who was also standing in the pulpit. John Doane then grabbed a chair from his family's pew, placed it in the alley, and sat down. There he remained for a considerable time, relieved once for a few moments by Mrs. Doane. At about ten o'clock Doane again urged Oakes to go up into the pulpit; he attempted to do so, but again Israel Young asked him to forbear, and once more he retreated to the Doanes' pew. Whereupon at John Doane's request Oakes began to make "his public devotions," praying in a loud voice.

At this moment the major part of the congregation came through the door, and after them entered Mr. Sumner, followed by Samuel Smith and John Rich. Constable Barnabas Young then approached Oakes and requested him to cease his devotions. When Oakes ignored him he repeated his demand, laying his hand on Oakes' shoulder, which caused Oakes to fall silent. John Doane (who, we will recall, was a justice of the peace) then placed his chair against the foot of the pulpit stairs, reseated himself, and said in a loud voice, "I command the King's peace!" Then addressing Constable Young, "I require you in His Majesty's name to take care of such as are disorderly and make a disturbance."

The constable asked Doane to get out of the alley so that the minister might enter the pulpit, saying, "You are the only disorderly person." At the same time he "gently" laid one hand on Doane's shoulder and placed the other under his arm. Samuel Brown standing by the constable repeated the order. Finally Doane rose and stood to one side.

When he did so, Mrs. Doane reached across the alley, seized the door of the deacons' pew, and pulled it open across the aisle so as to bar Mr. Sumner's way, until one of the Mayos wrenched it from her hand and slammed it shut. As Sumner walked by Mrs. Doane shook her fist under his nose and told him he had "the impudence of the Devil," and then emphasized her anger by knocking chairs about.

Thus at last Mr. Sumner ascended into the pulpit and delivered his sermon. There is no mention in any of the accounts of whether the Oakeses and the Doanes stayed to hear it.

On August 21, about five weeks later, Benjamin Wadsworth and Henry Flynt of Harvard College wrote to George Williamson that Mr. Sumner would not be accepting the call to Billingsgate and that the precinct need not expect further assistance from Harvard College. The inhabitants of Billingsgate, they advised, "had best procure some untitled minister near to you."

The confrontation of July 16 had by no means put the precinct in possession of the meeting house. Israel Young and Elisha Eldridge found a Mr. Taylor who was willing to consider a call to Billingsgate, but when they brought him to the meeting house in September they once again found Oakes refusing to yield the pulpit and the committee was obliged to take Mr. Taylor away to conduct a service in a private house.

THE GENERAL COURT VINDICATES THE INHABITANTS OF BILLINGSGATE

A precinct meeting on August 14, even before the committee had learned of Mr. Sumner's refusal, voted, first, to petition the General Court for assistance and, second, to build a new meeting house which would be the property of the precinct. Appeal to the General Court was

indeed the only remaining recourse for either party. Early in October the Oakes faction took the initiative by sending to Governor Dummer and the Court a petition alleging misappropriation of monies, signed by Richard Arey, Joseph Atkins, Thomas Atkins, John Atwood, Isaac Doane, John Doane, Thomas Gross, Abiah Harding, and Thomas Newcomb. Their opponents answered with a counter petition dated October 10, 1727 and signed by George Williamson and others.
The Court referred both petitions to the next session. Meanwhile the Court of General Sessions in Barnstable rejected Oakes' latest suit for payment of his salary, and on the same day, October 3, the Barnstable Grand Jury indicted the Oakeses and the Doanes for having on July 16 obstructed John Sumner from preaching and for breach of the sabbath and disorderly conduct.

In preparation for the hearing of the petitions by the General Court, the anti-Oakes party caused some nine affidavits to be sworn relating to the events of July 16 and of September 24 (the barring of Mr. Taylor from the meeting house). On November 22 John Doane and Josiah Oakes made depositions in reply to the allegations contained in George Williamson's petition. Joseph Lord, John Rich, and Sarah Covel also signed depositions on incidents related to the case.

Finally on December 2 the General Court issued its verdict, ruling that the inhabitants of the precinct had contracted with Mr. Oakes only from year to year and had expressed their desire that he should no longer continue as their minister. The Court therefore ordered that "Mr. Oakes Proceed no further in the Work of the Ministry in the said Precinct, and that the Inhabitants forthwith provide some suitable Person to Officiate as Minister there. And ... that the ... Inhabitants make just and speedy payment of what Money remains due him for his Service ... to May last 1727 ... at the rate of Eighty Pounds per Annum."

Thus ended the career of Josiah Oakes. The following February in 1728 a committee representing the proprietors of the meeting house, John Doane, Isaac Baker, and Israel Young, met with a committee of non-proprietors, Isaac Doane, Samuel Smith, and Eleazer Hamblin, and agreed that the meeting house would be leased to the committee of non-proprietors, who would pay for its maintenance.

After having endured what the General Court called the "very heavy and extraordinary troubles and grievances respecting the preaching of Mr. Josiah Oakes," the inhabitants found it difficult to find even an "untitled minister," as Harvard College had suggested. They extended calls to the Reverend Mr. David Hall in April 1728 and to Mr. Ezra Witmarsh in February 1729, but to no avail. Finally in January 1730 they voted to tender a call to the Reverend Mr. Isaiah Lewis, who did accept and who was to serve Billingsgate faithfully for many years.

Eventually, after prolonged debate as to the most convenient location, the vote of the August 1727 precinct meeting was carried out and a new meeting house was completed in 1740 at the head of Duck Creek on the King's Highway and adjacent to a new burying ground.

On September 12, 1728 John Doane had advertised his house on Chequesset Neck for sale in the *Boston Newsletter.* Whether he found no buyer or whether reasons of which we are ignorant intervened, he remained in Billingsgate a few years more. On September 4, 1731 Hannah Doane "was seized with a Fit of an Apoplexy" and died in her sixty-fifth year. She was buried a few yards from her namesake, little Hannah Oakes, who had lived only a few days longer than one month. Hannah Doane's obituary printed in the *Boston Newsletter* alluded obliquely to Billingsgate's troubled history: "Notwithstanding the Ill-Will which many have manifested to her Reproach, [she] is acknowledged to have been a woman ready to do Deeds of Charity, even to her Enemies; and it may well be thought made Conscience thereof, and had a serious regard to the Glory of GOD, and the things of another World." Not four months later Josiah Oakes followed her to the grave and was buried beneath a handsome tombstone close to those of the two Hannahs and his father. His epitaph was more succinct than Hannah Doane's obituary but reflected equally the tribulations of the precinct: "The memory of the Just however treated is blessed."

John Doane's career did not end with the deaths of his wife and of Oakes. He left Billingsgate in 1732 to settle in Hull, where he remained for ten years and where he married his third wife, Jane Baxter, by whom he had another son and four daughters. In 1742 he moved to Boston and died there in 1755 at the age of ninety-one, a wealthy man.

The cases of Samuel Osborn and Josiah Oakes were demonstrations of the basic instability of the ecclesiastical order in southeastern Massachusetts commencing in 1717 with the death of Samuel Treat. Ministerial unity was broken, and there was great uncertainty over what rules were to govern relationships between churches. A divided clergy found themselves unable to control deviant churches and to resolve disputes within congregations. Besides the Osborn and Oakes cases there were those of Benjamin Fessenden of Sandwich, of Daniel Greenleaf of Yarmouth, who sued his parish over his salary, and Josiah Marshall of Falmouth, who was dismissed for wife beating – to name only a few.[12]

The issues were not doctrinal. "In the entire fifty years between 1691 and the Great Awakening only one minister in southeastern Massachusetts got into serious trouble with his church over matters of doctrine – Samuel Osborn of Eastham. "[13] The conflicts were rather essentially political, but of two sorts: On the one hand, there were the politics of church government. These were the paramount concerns of Nathaniel Stone in both the Osborn and the Oakes cases. As a strong proponent of an educated clergy, doctrinal orthodoxy, Calvinistic predestination, and strict church discipline, he sternly opposed arguments for ecclesiastical democracy, church autonomy, or heterodoxy. In his election sermon, "Rulers Are a Terror, Not to Good, But Evil workers," preached before Governor Shute in 1720, he said that the civil powers of government are the "Ordinance of God." He entered the fray against the ordination of Osborn because he believed Osborn had not studied divinity "in order to the ministry," had not been disciplined for fornication, and was dangerously heterodox and Arminian in his theology. But his essential objection, as he stressed in "Rulers Are a Terror," was against the democratic folly of the people of

Eastham in "choosing Ministers according to their vain Fancies, without regard to the Civil Law, or Scripture, or Scriptural Qualifications."

Having jumped into the defense of Hannah Doane against Osborn and the deacons of Eastham, he was committed to the cause of Josiah Oakes. But in any case he would have stood by a graduate of Harvard College, fully qualified in theology by his M.A. degree and a member of the Boston establishment, against the democratic rebellion led by Billingsgate yeomen.

These were not, however, the politics of Billingsgate. The petitions to Governor Dudley in 1711 against the division of common lands in Billingsgate to the detriment of the settlers and native Indians like the petition of 1718 for the incorporation of Billingsgate as the town of Poole had a different character. Their force was essentially democratic in that it was directed toward the defense of common local interests that were being submerged in the over-extended townships which the seventeenth-century colonies had established. Though John Doane was no doubt acting out of political ambition and a vain desire to be the Squire of Billingsgate, he was, initially at least, an authentic champion of the farmers, fishermen, and whalers of Billingsgate, whose will was to govern themselves free of outside influences, burdensome taxes, and wearisome journeys to the meeting house by the Town Cove in Eastham. But when it came to accepting the Squire's wrong-headed choice of a minister, the same independent spirit united virtually the entire community in rebellion against what the people saw as autocratic rule. The Squire's authority, which had seemed so strongly rooted in the ground of tradition, was revealed to be a frail reed when not supported by the popular will. It is also significant that both times the inhabitants of Billingsgate took a stand for self-rule – for the right to be a separate precinct and for the right to have a minister of their own choice – they were ultimately supported by the General Court of Massachusetts. This was still a stratified society in which distinctions were carefully made between yeomen and gentlemen, between those addressed as squire, lieutenant, or Mr., or simply by their Christian names. But the tide had turned, notably in Billingsgate.

Chapter IV

BLESSINGS AND AFFLICTIONS, 1730-1763

By the ordination of Isaiah Lewis in 1730 the precinct was at last allowed surcease from internal dissension, but it was to face in the subsequent course of the century problems even more serious of an economic and political order.

The sandy hills and kettle holes of the high plain extending from Blackfish Creek north to the Pamet River presented dry, steep, unstable slopes poorly suited to the growing of crops. Only the salt meadows, the bottoms of kettle holes, and the narrow hollows watered by intermittent rivulets could grow the hay, corn, rye, and other crops the settlers attempted. They did better raising horses, cattle, sheep, and swine, all of which could be turned loose to feed themselves on beach grass or whatever vegetation they could find in the sedge meadows and cutover woodlands. But the land could not long stand up to such abuse, especially not to close grazing and rooting by half-starved sheep and swine. As the ground cover was destroyed, the thin top soil dried to a dark powder that blew away under the mildest breeze, exposing the yellow sand beneath, which the Atlantic gales drove and drifted into huge dunes that even the deep-rooted beach grass could not hold in place. The full effects of deforestation and overgrazing were not perceived until about 1740, but long before then the inhabitants had come to understand that what wealth they were to gain they must wrest from the sea.

THE BOUNTY OF THE SEA

The Plymouth colonists had fished the waters of Billingsgate since before 1650, but it was Cape Cod (as Provincetown and the Province Lands were first called) with its deep, well protected, and accessible harbor that quickly developed as a port for vessels engaged in taking finfish. Oysters and whales were to be the special resources of Billingsgate.

As we have noted, since the 1670s it had been necessary to defend the lucrative oyster beds against exploitation by "foreigners" from other towns. Quahogs and soft-shell clams were not in the seventeenth and eighteenth centuries commercial crops, for they could not be shipped like oysters, which stay alive in their shells for months if kept cool and which could also be pickled and sent in casks to the West Indies to feed the blacks.

Whaling was even more profitable. For reasons still not clearly understood, blackfish, a species of small cetacean also known as pilot whales or grampuses, frequently enter Billingsgate Bay, strand when the tide goes out, and die, sometimes in great numbers. It was such a beached blackfish that the exploring Pilgrims saw the Nauset Indians cutting up that cold day in December of 1620.

Larger species of whales – right whales, humpbacks, and others– congregated in the abundant feeding grounds in Cape Cod Bay and over Stellwagen Bank north of the Cape. Ezra Stiles recorded in his diary in 1762 that one Captain Atkins, a Truro man about sixty years old, told him "that he had seen as many whales in Cape Cod [Provincetown] harbor at one time as would have made a bridge from the end of the Cape to Truro shore, which is seven miles across and could require two thousand whales." Forty years ago, he told Stiles, Truro whalers took seventy to a hundred whales in the bay every season."

Under the statutes enacted by the Colony of New Plymouth drift whales cast up on a beach or found floating within a mile of shore belonged to the town. It was no doubt such whales – blackfish and sometimes larger species – that the first settlers in Billingsgate and Eastham exploited. Whether all inhabitants shared equally in the bounty is, however, uncertain. We find, for instance, in the Eastham town-meeting records that "About the 3d of November 1684 there was reported a whalefish ashore on the backside [ocean beach] and that John Snow, Josiah Cook, and Stephen Hopkins had cutt it up." They were obliged, the record shows, to surrender to the town the blubber they had stripped from the carcass.

The inhabitants of Billingsgate did not long remain content with the drift whales the waves might bring ashore. They soon began to pursue blackfish and larger whales in the harbor and beyond Billingsgate Point out in Cape Cod Bay, either driving their prey onto the flats or harpooning them and towing them ashore. In these endeavors they were assisted by the Punonakanit Indians of Billingsgate, the Nausets of Eastham, and the Potanumaquits of Harwich, who had been pursuing whales in dugout canoes for uncounted centuries and were expert harpooners. From these whaling "voyages," as they were called, the captured leviathans were hauled on the beach at Great Island or Lieutenant's Island, where "whale houses" had been erected in which the English and Indians stored their gear and tried the blubber in great iron trypots over wood fires. The Indians either went on their own voyages or hired out as harpooners or steersmen for the less experienced English crews organized by the townsmen. Under the date of 1710 in the Eastham records we find, for instance, that "the town voted to give unto Joseph Merrick the money which he engaged to pay for Indians that went in his employ a whaling at the Great Island at Billingsgate in the years 1707 and 1708, which is about 16 shillings."

Although captured whales were surely brought ashore at many locations, the best places were Great Island, which had beaches on both harbor and bay, and Lieutenant's Island, well located for the whaling grounds to the south, for both were in the early years covered with woods providing a plentiful supply of fuel. It was probably for these reasons that during all the seventeenth century both islands were reserved as common lands, Lieutenant's Island being set apart, by law if not in practise, for the support of the ministry.

Since these two islands were valued town assets, it was natural that when in 1691 Eastham was asked to contribute eighty-six pounds to the New Plymouth Colony's expenses for sending a delegation to London to attempt to regain the charter revoked by William and Mary, the selectmen decided to raise the money by mortgaging the two islands for the needed sum. John Freeman, one of the original Purchasers, provided the capital.

It was apparent by the first decade of the new century that whaling voyages could not continue to land on Lieutenant's Island and Great Island without some sort of regulation by the town. The problem was faced by the April 1707 town meeting, which enacted regulations on the landing of whaling boats on both islands and the cutting of wood by the crews. In order to tax the "foreigners" from other towns who were profiting from the Billingsgate whale fishery, it was voted that the harpooner or steersman of each boat was to pay two shillings for every member of his crew who was not an inhabitant of the town of Eastham, whether he were English or Indian.

The enforcement of these regulations proved difficult, so in August 1708 John Paine was instructed to see that they were obeyed. Then in May 1710 Isaac Pepper was given the policing power for two years and was promised one quarter of all the fees he collected. It appears, however, that neither Paine nor Pepper had much success in collecting the fees due, for in 1712 the town meeting abandoned the attempt at enforcement and voted "that there should be no persons persecuted in the law in the town's behalf for any arearage not paid by persons sitting down at Great Island at Billingsgate on whaling voyages."

The division of the common woodlands and meadows on Lieutenant's Island into large grants to individual inhabitants, voted in 1704 and substantially carried out by 1711, and the division of Great Island among some 135 grantees, voted in 1711 and completed in 1715, had the effect of closing down these two islands as whaling stations. Because of the total deforestation that ensued they no longer could supply firewood for the trying of blubber. Moreover, having become parcels of private property, they could not serve as public landings where whaling voyages could "sit down." This resulted in the removal of the whale houses to Billingsgate Point, where if there was no wood there were probably more whales, and in the transfer of offshore whaling to that area. In 1738 the Eastham town meeting complained that "the only place [this] antient town hath to sit down for whaling is Billingsgate Beach Point, where the whale houses now stand."

It appears that for a time both English and Indians maintained houses on the point, but by 1753 competition for use of this whaling station began to develop between certain English and the Indians of Eastham and Harwich, called by the English "the Poranumaquut people." In October of that year the town meeting voted to choose an agent, Samuel Smith, to join with the Potanumaquut people and help them to draw up the petition they were planning to present to the General Court, on the condition that this petition first be brought before the town meeting for approval.

It was not until four years later, however, on December 12, 1757, that the Potanumaquut petition was presented to the General Court – without (so far as the record shows) having been approved by the Town Of Eastham:

> A Petition of Thomas Rolfe, and others, in Behalf of themselves and the other Indians inhabiting the Towns of Eastham and Harwich, in the County of Barnstable, complaining of the Encroachments of their English Neighbors on their Lands, especially those lying in Eastham, and known by the Name of Billingsgate Point or Islands, which are commodiously situated for Fishing and Whaling Business, and their refusing to allow them any Improvement thereof, whereby they are reduced to great Difficulties for their Support; and praying, that they may be put into Possession of their native Rights and Properties.

The Court ordered that "the adverse party" (the Town of Eastham) be served a copy of the petition and that it make answer and also that the Guardians of the Potanumaquut Indians be informed and advise the Court.

In March 1758 the Eastham town meeting took note of the problem by protesting that "the town or proprietors of Eastham had disposed of their lands from whence they used to follow the whale fishing [Great and Lieutenant's Islands], and that thereby are greatly distrest." Sylvanus Snow was appointed to reply for the town. There is no record of the response or of whatever action the General Court took, if any. No doubt the gradual disappearance of both the whales and the Indians rendered the issue moot.

Meanwhile the more enterprising mariners of Billingsgate had long since ceased to pursue the diminishing numbers of whales in Cape Cod Bay. The skills and experience they had gained in the offshore fishery formed the foundation of a far more profitable deep-sea whaling industry. We have no record of the first oceangoing whaling ship to sail from Billingsgate, but we do know that by 1775 some 420 sailors, nine-tenths of the able-bodied men in the town, were manning between twenty and thirty whaling ships sailing as far as the coasts of Africa and bringing unheard of wealth to the port. Two leaders stood out among the whaling captains, Jesse Holbrook and Colonel Elisha Doane (1699-1759), the latter the second cousin of the departed Squire John Doane. A veteran of the Louisbourg expedition in 1744-1745, Elisha Doane had started his career as a harpooner and ended it as the principal financier of the Billingsgate whaling fleet and reputedly the second richest man in Massachusetts. He is said to have upheld his position by building a mansion in Billingsgate and buying his wife a fine carriage that kept getting stuck spoke-deep in the sandy Cape Cod roads.

All this prosperity was brought to a sudden halt by the Revolution. At the outbreak of hostilities the British navy established a tight blockade off Massachusetts ports, including Billingsgate. For seven years the town's proud whaling ships rotted at their moorings, and when the peace treaty was finally signed in 1783 there was no money left in the pockets of the former owners to rebuild the fleet. The port was very slow to recover, and when it did the seafaring men of the town who had not departed turned mainly to mackerel fishing and oystering. In 1802 there were only five whaling schooners sailing from Billingsgate Bay, and they frequently resorted to finfishing off Newfoundland or in the Straits of Belle Isle when the whales were scarce.[15]

THE SMALLPOX EPIDEMIC OF 1746-1748

The success of the whaling was balanced by a variety of afflictions, not the least of which was the smallpox epidemic of 1746-1748. The disease seems to have first appeared among the Indians of Billingsgate during the winter of 1746-1747. Samuel Smith, it is thought, took the lead in providing for their care, and on February 8, 1747 he applied to the General Court for relief from the expenses to which he had been put. A similar petition appears to have been presented to the Court by Zoheth Smith. In any case, on February 26 the Court voted that the province tax to be collected in Eastham was to be turned over to the selectmen to be distributed proportionately among the several families afflicted by smallpox: including Indians. On August 27 of the following summer Zoheth Smith and Elisha Holbrook on behalf of the North Precinct (Billingsgate) presented another petition to the Court, "representing their distress'd State by the spreading of the Small-Pox in that Parish." A special committee of the Court was appointed and as a result on September 1 it was voted that vessels sailing from Billingsgate to Boston would be required to present at Castle William in Boston Harbor a certificate signed by the Reverend Isaiah Lewis, Captain Elisha Doane, and Mr. Edward Righley attesting that the ship and its passengers, crew, and cargo were free from infection.

The care and support of the sick families impoverished by being unable to work continued to be a grave problem. On January 13, 1748 the town meeting voted to raise fifty pounds by an assessment on the estates of the ratable inhabitants to be "paid out to those persons ... that by reason of the late smallpox are become so poor as not to be able to pay the charge of their own or their relations' attendance and charge of sickness of said distemper." In May it was voted "that they that had the small pox at Billingsgate pay the charge of their tendance [care] that remains besides what the town has already paid."

There is no record of the number of deaths in Billingsgate, but it was certainly high, especially among the Indians. The epidemic must have been largely responsible for reducing the number of Billingsgate Indians to the pitiful handful that survived at the end of the century.

To the people of all the parishes of Eastham, beset by the recurring outbreaks of the disease and overwhelmed by realization of their impoverishment by uncontrollable erosion, the times seemed grim indeed. The August 22, 1748 town meeting chose a committee to draw up a petition to lay before the General Court "relating to the feeble and decaying circumstances of our town."

THE WASTING OF THE LAND

The most serious problem the inhabitants of Billingsgate faced during the colonial period, a problem whose damaging consequences were to extend down to the present day, was the destruction of the soil's productivity by eolian erosion and coastal flooding. This degradation of both the uplands and the wetlands was the penalty the settlers suffered for unregulated deforestation, failure to control fires, and inability or refusal to prevent overgrazing, particularly of sensitive areas such as coastal dunes.

Excessive deforestation was an abuse from which all the settled parts of New England began to suffer long before the end of the seventeenth century. The basis of the colonial economy was an extravagant consumption of wood, of which there appeared to be an inexhaustible supply. The inefficient colonial house consumed, according to one seventeenth-century estimate, forty cords of wood a year for heating and cooking; to build a house required 15-20,000 board feet; pine and oak were needed for shipbuilding; cedar for fencing; pitch pine for manufacturing turpentine; firewood for trying whale blubber and, until around 1778, for boiling seawater to produce salt. In addition there was the massive waste caused by the clear-cutting of broad roadways to allow the driving of great herds of sheep and cattle and by the systematic burning of common lands to provide pasturage. In the eighteenth century forest fires out of control sometimes burned for days or weeks until extinguished by rain.

It must also be remembered that not all of Cape Cod was forested before 1620. The Indians too had habitually burned the forest, in order to destroy the underbrush for better hunting, and they had totally cleared by burning large areas for the cultivation of corn. The Pilgrims found one such plot of about fifty acres in Truro. Of the total acres of the present Barnstable County it has been estimated that in 1620 1.5% were open corn lands, 2% abandoned corn lands partially reverted to forest, 61% forest affected by burning, and 1.5% swamps and barren sand dunes.

While the settlers on the mainland knew that behind them stretched a seemingly infinite virgin forest, when the inhabitants of Eastham and Billingsgate had lumbered the one- or two-milewide strip between the bay and the ocean they had exhausted their immediate forest resources and had to bring in firewood and lumber first from Scituate and later from Maine and New Hampshire.

The effects of the depletion of the forests of Eastham were being felt within thirty years of the first settlement. Numerous regulations were enacted beginning in the 1670s to prevent the taking, first, of pine knots and then of any kind of firewood or timber from the common lands. The task of policing the common proved, however, to be impossible, and, as we have seen, in 1704 and 1711 the town voted to proceed to a wholesale division of the common woodlands rather than to try to preserve them. This was the obvious and easy response to the political pressure for access to the town's wood, but it meant the abandonment of any effort to conserve the forest for future needs or for environmental benefits. Speculators bought up the divided woodlands and quickly lumbered them. Moreover as the shortage grew worse the value of wood rose, cutting was less and less selective, smaller trees were felled, and the ability of the forest to regenerate was diminished. By 1700, according to one authority, "forest renewal must have been at a standstill over the eastern part of the Cape."[16]

Deforestation reduced the sandy soil's capacity to absorb and retain rainfall, which in turn caused a lowering of the water table, the drying of intermittent and even perennial streams, and the parching of the topsoil. The most radical environmental impact occurred when these deforested lands were converted to pastures for horses, cattle, and especially sheep. It has been estimated that in 1660 (a mere forty years after the Pilgrims had landed) there were 7,000 to 10,000 sheep in Barnstable County. The largest flocks were in Eastham, Billingsgate, and Truro. The effects of this pasturing on the forests and cleared lands must have been heavy, especially when mixed grazing was the practise. Cattle prefer hardwood sprouts and browse on conifer seedlings only where other forage is scarce. Sheep, however, will feed on both broadleaf trees and conifers. Mixed grazing of both sheep and cattle can in a few years destroy all the young second growth of a cleared forest and eventually eliminate all trees, leaving only grasses, weeds, and shrubs of low palatability. This destruction in turn leads to more exposure and parching of the topsoil, which turns to powder, especially when the ground has been trampled by hundreds of sharp hooves. Under the strong prevailing winds the topsoil blew away, leaving exposed the glacial sand, which began to drift into dunes. Thus forest floors were buried under barren sand, sometimes ten or more feet deep. Whenever fires occurred, the process of desertification speeded up.

Overgrazing was even more disastrous in its effect on coastal dunes. The horses, cattle, and sheep feeding on the beach grass and whatever shrubs had established themselves destroyed the network of roots that was holding the sand in place, causing the dunes to migrate and be broken open by blowouts. Erosion by both wind and waves was increased by the trampling hooves of the animals. The result was that during winter storms at high tides the waves broke through the blowouts and created washovers, covering the meadows behind the dunes with sand, destroying vegetation with salt, and turning freshwater meadows into salt marshes. Thus many meadows granted in the early years were destroyed by what the settlers apparently regarded as acts of God. In the course of time, however, the destruction caused by grazing stock on coastal dunes came to be understood, and the towns of Barnstable County belatedly tried to protect their shorelines.

By 1740 the cumulative effects of deforestation and intensive mixed grazing had become so great that hundreds of acres had been degraded into virtual deserts. In fact the inhabitants of Billingsgate even feared that the clouds of sand blowing off Great Island and Billingsgate Beach might fill in the harbor and make it too shallow for vessels to navigate and anchor. The people of Barnstable County, and especially the inhabitants of Eastham, finally became aware of the seriousness and extent of the problem. They perceived that they were suffering from two kinds of destruction of agricultural land: one, which they called "broken lands," occurred in inland areas from loss of topsoil and the development of sand dunes; the other, along what they called the "Western Shore," consisted in the destruction of barrier beaches and coastal dunes and the invasion of the sea and sand over meadowlands and other poorly protected nearshore areas. The most serious case of the second danger was the damage being done to Great Island and Billingsgate Beach, lying between Billingsgate Bay and Cape Cod Bay.

The May 1740 Eastham town meeting "voted that the Selectmen ... take a valuation of their judgment of the damage done in and to said town by the Sea, fires, winds, and sands destroying such great quantities of their meadow ground and land and firewood and fencing stuff and exhibit the same under their hands by a petition to the Representative of said town in order for him to lay the same before the Great and General Court for their consideration for some abatement in said town's province tax next."

Under the political constitution of the Province of Massachusetts the towns were obliged to turn to the General Court for solutions to (or alleviation of) many of their local problems by either tax abatements, special appropriations, special legislation, or the appointment of ad hoc investigative committees. No tax abatement having been granted in 1740 to compensate Eastham for the damage to the town's lands, the December 1741 town meeting named Ralph Smith and Samuel Freeman a committee instructed to draw up a petition to the General Court "relating to the great destruction that is lately made in said town's medow ground being destroyed by the sea breaking in upon and covering up the same in so great a manner with sands, and also the destruction [of] said Town's firewood by running fires, and also to do what is proper for preventing Billingsgate beach being destroyed." On the recommendation of this committee the town, besides repeating its request for a tax abatement, petitioned for a special act designed to preserve Great Island and Billingsgate Beach.

Efforts to protect private and common lands from incursions of freely ranging stock of all kinds and to prevent the creation of "broken lands" had begun long before 1740 and continued until the Revolution, demonstrating the inability of both the towns and the province to manage the environment. In 1725 and 1727 the Eastham town meeting had tried ineffectually to enact regulations on the driving of the large flocks of sheep herded every spring for shearing. In the June 1741 town meeting inhabitants raised the problem of swine going at large and the need to prevent cattle from breaking out of private lands into the common sedge flats. At the May 1747 meeting the problem of "broken land in the middle part of ... town" was debated and the meeting voted to "chuse a number of men to impound all such sheep as they should find going at large on said broken land."

In March 1747 an ad hoc town committee presented a petition to the General Court for a special act "to prevent the destruction of a large Body of Meadow and Sedge Ground in said Town by feeding Horses and Cattle thereon." A committee of the Court was ordered to prepare a bill "to relieve the Petitioners, as also the Inhabitants of Barnstable," but no such legislation was ever introduced, no doubt because of the difficulty in drawing up effectual regulations of this sort. The town meeting of the following May (1748) was evidently trying to cope with the same continuing problems in discussing "broken land in the middle part of town" and voting to "chuse a number of men to impound all such sheep as they should find going at large on said broken land."

The town meeting of May 1749 voted to petition the Court for "liberty to stop all lanes or ways that lead to broken land in the middle part of town by fencing across them by gates or bars." The next month another ad hoc committee led by one James Higgins and representing proprietors of common and undivided lands and beaches in the southeastern part of Eastham petitioned the General Court for an act forbidding the grazing of cattle or horses on these lands. Again the effort for relief by the Court came to nothing. Two years later, in March 1751, the town voted to exercise its own authority to bar by gates the ways leading to the "broken land" in the middle part of town. Ineffectual discussions of the "broken land" problem and the control of unfenced stock continued to occupy town meetings up to at least 1757.

In the 1750s the major attention, however, was directed to the problem of the "Western Shore," presumably the bay shore from Silver Spring Harbor south to the Harwich line. The May 1754 meeting debated "What shall be thought proper concerning the Western shore both lands and meadows?" A proposal was made to block all ways leading to the shore, but a motion to petition the General Court to enact such a prohibition failed, no doubt because the inhabitants had learned that it was hopeless to expect effective remedial legislation from Boston. In March 1762 the town meeting appointed a committee of five to make a recommendation on the fencing of the Western Shore "in order to keep creatures from feeding thereon," and the following June it appointed agents to work with the town of Harwich in a joint undertaking to fence off the Western Shore.

One act for the protection of "broken land" was passed by the General Court in March 1768, after the precinct of Billingsgate had been incorporated as the District of Wellfleet. It was entitled "An Act to Prevent Damage Being Done on Bound Brook Island and Griffith's Island, within the District of Wellfleet, by Cattle, Horse Kind, and Sheep Feeding Thereon." The destruction of ground cover in this area must have been extensive in 1768, and it may have continued largely unchecked into the nineteenth century, for even in the early twentieth century large expanses of both islands were still bare of even the smallest trees.

In the same year, 1768, agents from the towns of Eastham, Chatham, and Harwich and the District of Wellfleet presented a petition to the General Court "setting forth the Danger of their lands being ruined by the wind blowing on the sands." The Court duly appointed a committee "instructed to view the Lands of the whole County of Barnstable at the Expence of the several Towns in said County."

The most notable effort by the General Court and the inhabitants of Billingsgate and Eastham to use legislation to prevent environmental damage was in the case of the Great Island, Great Beach Hill, Little Beach Hill, and Billingsgate Beach area. Subsequent to the division of Great Island in 1715 and after virtually all the trees on it had been cut, the ownership of most of the island had passed, as we have noted, to Samuel Smith. In the 1730s, or perhaps earlier, it became the practice of owners of horses, cattle, and sheep to turn their stock loose on Great Island and the other islands and the beach to the south.

It soon became obvious that these animals were doing great damage by browsing on the grass, shrubs, and tree seedlings growing among the stumps left after the clear-cutting of the woods that had once covered the uplands and by feeding on the beach grass that anchored the dunes of the long tombola or sand spit known as Billingsgate Beach. Contemporary accounts tell of great clouds of sand blowing out over the harbor. A hypothetical reconstruction indicates that on the uplands of Great Island and the smaller Great Beach Hill and Little Beach Hill the denuded slopes quickly lost their topsoil under the strong prevailing southwest and northwest winds. The underlying sands of the glacial till then began to drift and form dunes, which migrated from west to east until they reached the tops of the scarps facing the harbor, from where the sand blew out over the shallow waters. Farther south the barrier dunes that had long defended the extended tombolo of Billingsgate Beach, now stripped of their deep-rooted beach grass, drifted eastward and suffered overwashes. Multiple breaches were probably created by heavy surf and soon widened into sloughs cut through the tombola. What alarmed the people of Billingsgate was not the loss of productive land, which was negligible, but the threat to the harbor – the danger, they imagined, that the bulwark of islands and beach might literally be blown into the roadstead it had for centuries protected. Another and more immediate imagined threat was that the wind-blown sand might bury the oyster beds.

Since grazing stock could be fenced off or impounded only under authorization by a special provincial act, the Eastham town meeting in December 1741 directed Ralph Smith and Samuel Freeman to draw up the petition to the General Court for the necessary legislation. Samuel Smith and John Holbrook, the principal owners of Great Island, likewise presented a supporting petition.

The Court responded promptly by passing on June 22, 1742 a bill entitled "An Act to Prevent Damage Being Done unto Billingsgate Bay in the Town of Eastham by Cattle and Horsekind and Sheep Feeding on the Beach and Islands Adjoining Thereto." We should note that the purpose of the act was to protect not the beach and the islands but the bay behind them, and also that the cause of the eolian erosion was clearly and correctly identified. The act provided that "no person shall presume to turn or drive any neat cattle or horsekind or sheep to or upon the islands or beach lying westerly of Billingsgate Bay and south of Griffens Island." Penalties (10 shillings per horse or head of cattle and 2/6 per sheep) were fixed; it was made lawful for any person to impound any animal found in violation of the act; and the town was directed to appoint enforcing officers.

Since the act ran for only five years, a bill to renew it for another ten years was passed in 1747. A petition by unnamed proprietors of

Billingsgate requesting defeat of the new act was for some reason presented (perhaps by owners of stock) to the Court in June 1747 but it had no influential backing and was rejected without debate.

Two years later in March 1749 Samuel Smith and others presented a petition to amend the act of 1747, and as a result a bill entitled "An Act in Addition to the Act Intitled an Act to Prevent Damage Being Done unto Billingsgate Bay in the Town of Eastham by Cattle and Horse Kind and Sheep Feeding on the Beach and Islands Adjoining Thereto" was passed in April 1750. This act required Smith and the other proprietors to "make and maintain a good and sufficient fence across the north part of ... Great Island" (presumably across the Gut) and "also build a House on said Island and settle and keep a family therein" for a period of seven years. In return Smith was granted permission to keep a limited number of cattle on Great Island during certain periods of the year, and also a cow for the use of the family who were to occupy the house.

From the provisions of the act it is obvious that there was no dwelling on Great Island previous to March 1749 (the date on which the seven-year permission began); the building here authorized was almost certainly the one which was later occupied by the so-called Great Island Tavern.

There is, it is true, archaeological evidence of at least three other eighteenth-century structures on Great Island in addition to the "tavern": two reported by the National Park Service archaeologists, one designated site C10 near the shallow pond in the center of the island and the other, C11, near the Herring River. A third site, which may be designated C11A, is located some distance east of C11. Since the excavations of Cl0 and C11 in 1969 or 1970 seem to have been limited to a single test pit at each site, since no catalog exists of the finds at either,[17] and since C11A, though definitely dating from the eighteenth century, is quite small in area, it seems likely – at least until we have more evidence – that these are sites of subsidiary activities related to the "tavern," perhaps a facility for drawing fresh water from the nearby pond and wharves or sheds on the Herring River.

It Is clear from later legislation that the main structure, thoroughly excavated in 1969 and 1970, was intended initially for use not as a public tavern but as housing for the family of the caretaker whom Smith was required to employ to police the island. The conversion (and perhaps enlargement) of the original dwelling into a tavern, which does indeed seem probable from archaeological studies and the oral tradition, must tentatively be dated no earlier than the late 1750s. In June 1756, in anticipation of the expiration of the act of 1747, Samuel Smith once more petitioned for extension of the legislation. The new act, passed in February 1757, renewed the provisions of the two previous versions with only insignificant changes and included again the construction of a "good and sufficient fence" across the Gut and the requirement that Smith "keep a House and family on said island," thus apparently establishing a terminus a quo for the tavern. These dates for the construction of the dwelling (1749 or 1750) and its conversion to a tavern seven or more years later are not radically inconsistent with the estimated pipe-stem mean date of 1740 and the ceramic mean date of 1742, estimated by Synenki and Charles (1984) from data they concede are short of optimum reliability. In any case, the late-seventeenth- and early-eighteenth-century dates formerly attributed to the "tavern" do not seem tenable.[18]

It appears that storms during 1756-1757 caused considerable damage to the fence, so that in November 1757 Smith petitioned the Court to repeal this requirement, writing, "It [is] altogether impracticable to make a fence that will stand against the Sea, Tide, and Ice." The Court complied, passing on the last day of December 1757 "An Act for Altering a Clause of an Act Made in the Thirtieth Year of His Present Majesties Reign Intitled an Act to Prevent Damage Being Done unto Billingsgate Bay ... [etc.]"

Lastly, in 1763 Samuel Smith was allowed to bring before the Court a bill for still another amendment to the most recent act entitled, "An Act for Altering a Clause in an Act Made in the Thirtieth Year of His Late Majesty King George the Second, Intitled An Act to Prevent Damage Being Done unto Billingsgate Bay .. , [etc.]"

The inhabitants of the town and precinct showed from the 1740s through the 1760s a keen interest in the strict enforcement of these several acts and amendments. Their concern was undoubtedly caused, as we have indicated, by the belief that erosion of the beach and islands was a very real threat to the usefulness of the harbor. Even before the enactment of the first act, the June 1741 town meeting had discussed "what may be proper to prevent creatures being drove on Billingsgate Beach or going there." The town meeting records of March 1746 and March 1747 contain significant entries: "Then [the meeting] chose to put the law in practice relating to creatures going on Billingsgate Beach Benjamin Young;" and "Then chose to put the law in force relating to creatures going at large at Billingsgate Beach – Capt. Samuel Smith." At the May 1749 meeting, for reasons unexplained, the majority voiced strong dissatisfaction with the way those responsible were protecting the harbor: "Voted that Stephen King, David Vickery, and Benjamin Young should be the men to see the law put in force relating to Billingsgate beach and ... voted that Samuel Smith, Esq. should be dismissed from taking care of Billingsgate beach – and it was voted that Capt. Elisha Doane and Ezekiel Holbrook should be prosecuted for not taking their oath to see the law put in execution relating to Billingsgate beach."

Samuel Smith's petition in 1756 for the renewal of the act with a provision for the grazing of a few cattle on Great Island led the town meeting to approve a motion to specify precisely how many animals he could bring on the island and between what dates, and at the same time to reaffirm the town's power to appoint an officer to inspect the beach and the islands.

The next year, in accordance with the provisions of the new act of 1757, the town chose Simeon Smith "to take care of Great Island according to the late act," and voted detailed provisions allowing Samuel Smith to introduce a few horses and heifers as part of his allowed herd and appointing Ephraim Covel and Jonas Young as inspectors of the island. From this year forward to 1763 the Eastham town meeting regularly appointed a person "to keep the law for Billingsgate Beach."

The continual renewals and amendments of the legislation written to protect Billingsgate Bay and also the continuing concern with enforcement suggest that the prevention of overgrazing on the islands and beach was perceived as both necessary and effective. It may therefore be supposed that the upland portions of the islands gradually were regaining enough shrubs and second-growth trees to stabilize the surface and prevent the formation of moving dunes and clouds of sand. It is likely, however, that the beach grass never wholly reestablished itself the length of the beach from Little Beach Hill south to Billingsgate Point. This lack of ground cover, but possibly also new alongshore current patterns, may have contributed to the formation of the Slue which was developing between Billingsgate Point and the rest of the beach to the north, thereby turning the point into an island. There is evidence in the 1757 Potanumaquut petition, which referred to "Billingsgate Point or Islands," that the Slue (or slues) had already broken through, at least intermittently, by the middle of the eighteenth century.

The efforts to prevent the formation of "broken land" appear, however, to have been largely ineffectual. Descriptions written by late-eighteenth-century and nineteenth-century travelers, early photographs, and the still persisting physical appearance of many sections of the Lower Cape give vivid representations of the treeless waste that the fatal combination of unrestricted deforestation and intensive multiple grazing created.

THE POLITICS OF GROWTH

Despite smallpox, erosion, the shortage of wood, and the exhaustion of the soil, Billingsgate continued to grow. The population of Eastham in 1644 was forty-nine. By 1650 there were an estimated 300 inhabitants in the entire township, and by 1684 the total was about 650. In 1700 the estimate was 850, and in 1725, 900. It is difficult to determine what fraction of the town's total population lived north of Indian Brook in Billingsgate at various stages in the hamlet's growth, but it appears probable that in 1700 the figure was about 200 and in 1725, 300. In

1764, after the District of Wellfleet had been established, there were 1331 inhabitants in Eastham and about 550 in Wellfleet.[19]

Two political problems became increasingly pressing after 1723. One issue was the creation of a county court conveniently located to serve the people of the Lower Cape towns; the other was the incorporation of Billingsgate as a town.

It was initially proposed that the towns of Harwich, Chatham, Eastham, Truro, and Provincetown form a new county. One of the articles on the warrant of the November 1734 town meeting was to name an agent to meet with representatives from the other four Lower-Cape towns to petition the General Court to this end. The effort did not succeed, but three years later, in 1737, Eastham with the support of the other towns petitioned the General Court "that two sessions of the Superior Court of Common Pleas and General Sessions of the Peace for the County of Barnstable be yearly held in Eastham," and that for this purpose a courthouse and prison be built in Eastham. The proposal was, however, rejected.

The effort to elevate Billingsgate to the status of a town made, however, more progress.

On December 12, 1737 Samuel Smith, "in the name and by order of the North Precinct" petitioned that the North Precinct of Billingsgate might "be erected into a distinct and separate township" with boundaries the same as those of the existing precinct. On May 15, 1738 the Eastham town meeting debated the North Precinct's proposal and voted a number of objections and reservations regarding the suggested boundary. Speakers pointed out that Eastham would lose about half its territory, plus the taxes being paid by the four families dwelling north of the precinct boundary who had been permitted in 1723 to remain members of the old first church in Eastham. It was argued that the remaining inhabitants of Eastham would be hard pressed to support the two churches at Herring Pond and Pochet. Moreover, objectors said, Eastham would lose Silver Spring Harbor, "the only harbor that the antient town of Eastham have or can have to harbor their vessels, take in loading or unload goods either to or from market." Besides, "the only place said ancient town hath to sit down for whaling is Billingsgate Beach point, where the whale houses now stand." The town meeting voted, nevertheless, that it would agree to a boundary line running from the point where the public road (the King's Highway) crossed Fresh Brook eastward to the "Backside sea" (the Atlantic Ocean) and westward by the thread of the brook into Silver Spring Harbor and thence by the middle of that harbor to Billingsgate Beach Point, reserving to the inhabitants of Eastham the right to whale from Billingsgate Point and to take oysters and seals from Billingsgate Bay. This proposed line running approximately due east and west lay about one mile north of the existing precinct boundary along Indian Brook and thence eastward to the Backside.

The Governor's Council agreed on June 14, 1738 that the petitioners might bring in a bill that the North Precinct "be erected into a separate and distinct Township" but only "agreable to the Bounds and Reservations and Provisos mentioned in a Vote of the Town of Eastham." With this the House concurred. Samuel Smith and his supporters, however, were apparently unwilling to accept this compromise and they dropped the initiative.

The second attempt was to establish Billingsgate not as a separate town but as a district. A district differed from a town principally in that it was represented jointly with the town of which it was a part by a single representative in the House of Representatives, but in other respects it enjoyed virtually all the powers and rights of a town. The petitioners left the boundary between Eastham and the new district the same as that of the existing precinct, that is, by the thread of Indian Brook and due east from its source to the ocean and due west from its mouth.

A petition to this effect was first presented to the Eastham town meeting on September 13, 1762 and was referred to a committee of ten, which reported on October 11. The meeting voted to agree to a boundary defined by the thread of Blackfish Creek and thence eastward to the ocean and westward across Billingsgate Bay, reserving to the inhabitants of both parts of the town the privileges of whaling, oystering, fishing, and "harboring" in all parts of Billingsgate Bay.

The precinct petitioners, headed by Elisha Doane, made their initial presentation to the General Court on January 19, 1763, proposing no change from the existing boundary of Indian Brook. This petition was referred to the Eastham town meeting, which on May 10 named Captain Solomon Pepper as the town's agent and appointed a committee of five to instruct him.

On June 2, Elisha Doane's petition to the Court and Captain Pepper's answer on behalf of the Town of Eastham were referred to a special committee charged to report back to the General Court. Here there is a gap in the record, but it is evident that Elisha Doane, the wealthy son of the late Colonel Elisha Doane, wielded more influence in the State House than did Solomon Pepper, the Eastham agent. On June 7 Elisha Doane was given liberty to bring in a bill, which was promptly passed by both the Governor's Council and the House of Representatives and was approved by the Governor on June 16, 1763. The southern boundary of the former precinct, Indian Brook, became the boundary between the new district and the remainder of Eastham. The line extended due east from the source of the stream to the ocean and due west from its mouth along a line that passed north of Billingsgate Point. Thus the inhabitants of Eastham continued to share with the Potanumaquut Indians the right to erect whale houses on the point, which perhaps by now was an island.

One curious but important detail remains to be recounted. The bill to create the new district when first read in the Court was entitled "An Act to Incorporate the North Precinct of Eastham into a District by the Name of [blank]." It was passed by both the Council and the House with the name of the new district still blank. Not until June 16, when the Governor affixed his signature to the act, was the name "Wellfleet" inserted in the title.

No one appears to have discovered any written evidence of how or why the name Wellfleet was chosen. Indeed there is not even an oral tradition to offer a clue, though there has been no lack of speculation. The name Billingsgate had continued to be appropriate because of the abundance of finfish and shellfish, but the word also had its other connotation. The fishwives of Billingsgate market in London had long been notorious for their foul mouths, and in the eighteenth century the word *billingsgate* denoted coarsely abusive language, as it still does today. Indeed it seems likely that by 1763 this pejorative meaning, which is well attested, was far more current in Massachusetts than the sense of fish market. Moreover it is more than possible that the legend of Hannah Doane's diatribes against the deacons of Eastham and her abuse of the unhappy John Sumner gave the name Billingsgate on the Lower Cape a special and humorous appropriateness that Elisha Doane and others did not relish. In fact, while the name Billingsgate continued in common use and can be found in official documents at least as late as 1756, it appears to have been declining in frequency, notably in town and state papers, yielding place frequently to the term "North Precinct." There clearly was agreement, in any case, that the new district deserved a new name.

It is equally clear that the sponsors of the new district had great difficulty in agreeing on what this new name should be, though we have no idea of the possibilities they considered. The inhabitants were too far removed from England to prefer a name associated with their ancestral origins, as the Pilgrims had done in naming Plymouth, Sandwich, Falmouth, Barnstable, Chatham, Eastham, Truro, Yarmouth, and Harwich. Alternatively they might have chosen the name of some respected figure, as was done in the cases of Dennis and Brewster, but Billingsgate's stormy history had enshrined no one as a revered hero. Eventually the leaders of the would-be district settled on "Wellfleet." The name had never been applied to the Billingsgate area, and there was no town by this name in England. Wellfleet, frequently spelled Wallfleet, was, however, the name given to a portion of a tidal creek south of the River Crotch in Essex on the east coast of England, variously identified as part of the River Roach a half mile east of Paglesham Point or as a section of the appropriately named New

England Creek between New England Island and Havengore Island. These tidal estuaries produced excellent oysters, and in the eighteenth century Wallfleet or Wellfleet oysters commanded top prices in European fish markets, including, of course, Billingsgate Market in London. We may not unreasonably suppose that the founders of the new district hoped that by giving to the district and the harbor the name of Wellfleet they could in good conscience claim to be marketing Wellfleet oysters – and at prices inflated by the reputation of their English namesakes.

After the outbreak of the Revolution the General Court voted to raise all districts in the Commonwealth to the status of towns. Thus the hamlet of Billingsgate became in 1775 – not in 1763 – at last the Town of Wellfleet.

NOTES

1. George Mourt, *A Journal of the Pilgrims at Plymouth: Mourt's Relation: A Relation or Journal of the English Plantation Settled at Plymouth in New England by Certain English Adventurers Both Merchants and Others*, ed. Dwight B. Heath (New York: Corinth Books, 1963).
2. Enoch Pratt, *A Comprehensive History, Ecclesiastical and Civil, of Eastham, Wellfleet and Orleans, County of Barnstable, Mass. From 1644 to 1844* (Yarmouth, 1844), pp. 11-12.
3. Francis Baylies, *An Historical Memoir of the Colony of New Plymouth.* From *the Flight of the Pilgrims into Holland in the Year 1608, to the Union of the Colony with Massachusetts in 1692* ... (Boston, 1866), pp219-20
4. George D. Langdon, Jr., *Pilgrim Colony: A History of New Plymouth, 1620-1691* (New Haven, 1966), pp. 39 ff. *Records of the Colony of New Plymouth* (Boston, 1855-1861) II, 4, Dec. 1, 1640.
5. *Records of the Colony of New Plymouth,* II, 161-62, Oct. 2, 1650; III, 53, June 6, 1654; IV, 185, June 3, 1668; *Laws, 1632-1682,* pp. 236- 37.
6. See Erik Ekholm and James Deetz, "Wellfleet Tavern," *Natural History,* 20 (Aug.-Sept., 1971), 49-56.
7. Francis P. McManamon et al., "The Indian Neck Ossuary," *Chapters in the Archaeology of Cape* Cod, vol. 5 (U.S. Department of the Interior, Boston, 1986).
8. Daniel Gookin, "Historical Recollections of the Indians of New England," *Collections of the Massachusetts Historical Society for the Year 1792* (Boston: Re-Printed by Munroe and Francis, 1806), I, 197.
9. Thomas Hutchinson, *The History of the Colony and Province of Massachusetts-Bay,* ed. Lawrence S. Mayo (Cambridge, Mass., 1936), I,296.
10. Grimal Rawson and Samuel Danforth, [Account] in Nicholas Noyes, *New England's Duty and Interest* ... (Boston: Bartholomew Green and John Allen, 1698), p. 96.
11. *The Result of a Council Held at Billingsgate in Eastham, November* 8, *1720. With Illustrations of the Reasons against*

Joining with Eastham in *Calling a Council. And the Narrative of Hannah Doane, Briefly Giving an Account of the Proceedings of the Church Whereof She Was a Member, against Her; and the Occasion Thereof* (Boston, [1722]).

12. See John Michael Bumstead, "The Pilgrims' Progress: The Ecclesiastical History of the Old Colony, 1620-1775." Diss. Brown Univ. 1965.
13. *Ibid.,* p. 72.
14. Ezra Stiles, *Extracts from the Itineraries and Other Miscellanies of Ezra Stiles,* D.D., LL.D., *1755-1794, with a Selection from* His *Correspondence,* ed. Franklin D. Dexter (New Haven, 1916), pp. 168, 169.
15. Henry C. Kittredge, *Cape Cod: Its People and Their History* (Boston: Houghton Mifflin & Co., 1930), pp. 172, 187.
16. L. Stanford Altpeter, "A History of the Forests of Cape Cod." M.A. Thesis Harvard Univ. 1939, p 32.
17. Alan T. Synenki and Sheila Charles, *Archaeological Collections Management of the Great Island Tavern Site,* Cape *Cod National Seashore, Massachusetts.* ACMP Series No. 3. (Division of Cultural Resources, North Atlantic Regional Office, National Park Service, U.S. Department of the Interior, Boston, 1984), pp. ix, 3, 14, 71.
18. Ibid., pp. 7-8.
19. Altpeter, Appendix B.

Selected Bibliography

PRIMARY SOURCES

Manuscripts

Billingsgate (Hamlet). Indians. [Petition to John Doane.] [Dated] June 13, 1711. Massachusetts State Archives. Vol. 113, p. 607. Photocopy in Wellfleet Historical Society.

Billingsgate (Hamlet). Inhabitants. [Statement supporting Petition by John Doane to Governor Dudley, June 12, 1711.] Massachusetts State Archives. Vol. 113, p. 606. Photocopy in Wellfleet Historical Society.

Doane, John. [Petition] "To His Excellency Joseph Dudley ... Governor ... and Her Majesty's Council." June, 1711.] Massachusetts State Archives. Vol. 113, p. 608. Photocopy in Wellfleet Historical Society.

Eastham, Mass. "Record of Town Meetings in Eastham from 1654 to 1745." Eastham Town Hall.

———. "Records of Land and Meadow Grants, &c. of the Town of Eastham from 1654 to 1743." Eastham Town Hall.

Eastham, Mass. North Precinct. "Precinct Records, 1723-1763." Wellfleet Town Hall. Published: "Records of Wellfleet, Formerly the North Precinct of Eastham, Mass." *The Mayflower Descendant,* IV, 227-32; V, 96-99; VI, 51-54; VII, 231-35; VIII, 24-27; X, 152-54, 221-25; XI, 73-78; XIII, 184-89, 208-17.

Massachusetts. State Archives. Vol. l. Agriculture, 1644-1774, pp. 154, 155, 156, 157, 158, 158a, 159, 160, 182, 183, 184, 184 verso, 190, 191, 192, 200, 299, 300, 301, 302, 303, 304, 305, 325, 469, 470; Vol. 11. Ecclesiastical, 1679-1739, pp. 439, 439a, 439b, 440, 440a, 441, 441a, 442, 442a, 442b, 443, 444, 445, 445a, 446, 447, 447a, 448, 448a, 449, 449a, 450, 450a, 451, 452, 452a, 453,455, 455a, 456, 456a, 457, 457a, 458, 459, 459a, 460, 461,462, 462a, 463, 463a, 464,465, 465a, 481, 481a, 482,483, 483a, 483b; Vol. 115. Smallpox, p. 234.

Massachusetts. Suffolk County. Suffolk Court Files. Suffolk County Courthouse, Boston. Cases nos. 19536, 26274.

Printed

Boston News-Letter, July 17, 1719;Sept.18, 1728;Sept.30, 1731;Feb. 22,1733.

Bradford, William. *Of Plymouth Plantation, 1620-1647,* ed. Samuel Eliot Morison. New ed. New York: Knopf, 1952.

A *Church of Christ Vindicated.* A *Short and Plain Relation of Some Transactions* in *the South Church at Eastham, Forced into the Publick by Several Sallacious Pamphlets That Have Been Lately Published.* Boston: Thos. Fleet, [1724].

Danforth, Samuel. *See* Rawson, G., and Samuel Danforth.

Doane, Hannah. *See The Result of a Council Held at Billingsgate.*

Gookin, Daniel. "Historical Recollections of the Indians in New England." *Collections of the Massachusetts Historical Society. For the Year 1792.* Re-Printed by Munroe and Francis, 1806. I, 141-232.

Hutchinson, Thomas. *The History of the Colony and Province of Massachusetts-Bay ...* , ed. Lawrence S. Mayo. 3 vols. Cambridge, Mass., 1936.

Lord, Joseph. *The Great Privilege of Children of GOD, Is Their Liberty to Be Ever with Him . . . . Shewed* in *a Sermon Preached* in *the North Precinct of Eastham . . . on the 24th Day of the 12th Month . . . .* Boston, 1731.

Lord, Joseph, and Nathaniel Stone. *Additional Proposals for Convictions of the Churches.* 1729.

———. *The Veracity and Equity of the Members of the Council Held at Billingsgate in Eastham, 1720. Asserted* and *Maintained.* Boston: Thos. Fleet, 1723.

———. *See The Result of the Council Held at Billingsgate.*

Massachusetts (Province). Court of Admiralty. *The Trials of Eight Persons Indited for Piracy* &c. *of Whom Two Were Acquitted and the Rest Found Guilty ....* Boston: B. Green, 1718. (Trial of members of the crew of the pirate ship *Whidah,* Capt. Samuel Bellamy.)

Massachusetts (Province). General Court. *Acts and Resolves of Massachusetts Bay.* Boston, 1869-1922. Massachusetts (Province). General Court. House of Representatives. *Journals of the House of Representatives of Massachusetts . . . .* The Massachusetts Historical Society, 1919 ff.

Mourt, George. *A Jornal of the Pilgrims at Plymouth: Mourt's Relation: A Relation or Journal of the English Plantation Settled at Plymouth in New* England, *by Certain English Adventurers Both Merchants and Others,* ed. Dwight B. Heath. New York: Corinth Books, 1963.

New Plymouth (Colony). *Records of the Colony of New Plymouth, in New England* .... 12 vols. Boston: W. White, 1855-1861.
Osborn, Samuel. *The Case* and *Complaint of Mr. Samuel Osborn, Late of Eastham: As It Was Represented in a Letter to the Reverend Dr. Colman, to Be Communicated by Him to the Convention for Their Consideration.* Boston, 1743.
———. *See* A *Church of Christ Vindicated.*
Rawson, Grimal, and Samuel Danforth. [Account of Indians], pp. 88-99 in Nicholas Noyes. *New-Englands Duty and Interest, to Be a Habitation of Justice, and Mountain of Holiness* .... Boston: Bartholomew Green and John Allen, 1698. Republished as "Account of an Indian Visitation, AD. 1698." *Collections of the Massachusetts Historical Society.* X (1809), 129 ff.
The Result of a Council Held at Billingsgate in Eastham, November 8. *1720. With Illustration of the Reasons against Joining with Eastham in Calling a Council. And the Narrative of Hannah Doane, Briefly Giving an Account of the Proceedings of the Church Whereof She Was a Member, against Her; and the Occasion Thereof.* Boston: Tho. Flint, [1722].
Stiles, Ezra. *Extracts from the Itineraries and Other Miscellanies of Ezra Stiles ... with a Selection from His Correspondence,* ed. Franklin B. Dexter. New Haven: Yale Univ. Press, 1916.
Stone, Nathaniel. *Post-Script, in 1732, to Additional Proposals for Convictions of the Churches.* 1732.
———. *Rulers Are a Terror, Not to Good, but Evilworkers.* A *Sermon Preached before His Excellency Samuel Shute . . . on the Day of Election.* Boston, 1720.
———. *Serious Reflections on Late Publick Concernments* in *These Churches.* [1735].
———. Some *Things Briefly Offered for Information of the Churches.* [1721].
———. *See* Lord, Joseph, and Nathaniel Stone.
———. *See The Result of the Council Held at Billingsgate.*

SECONDARY SOURCES

Altpeter, L. Stanford. "A History of the Forests of Cape Cod." M.A. Thesis Harvard Univ. 1939.
Baylies, Francis. *An Historical Memoir of the Colony of New Plymouth, from the Flight of the Pilgrims* into *Holland in the Year* 1608, *to the Union of That Colony with Massachusetts* in *1692* .... 2 vols. Boston:

Wiggin and Lunt, 1866.
Bridenbaigh, Carl. "Yankee Use and Abuse of the Forest in the Building of New England, 1620-1660." *Proceedings of the Massachusetts Historcal Society,* 89 {1977), 3-35.
Brown, Robert Elden. *Middle-Class Democracy and the Revolution* in *Massachusetts, 1691-1780.* New York: Russell and Russell, (1968].
Bumstead, John Michael. "The Pilgrims' Progress: The Ecclesiastical History of the Old Colony, 1620-1775." 2 vols. Diss. Brown Univ. 1965.
Bushman, Richard L. *King and People in Provincial Massachusetts.* Chapel Hill: Univ. of North Carolina Press, 1985.
Clemensen, Berle. *Historic Resource Study. Cape Cod National Seashore, Massachusetts.* Denver Service Center, Historic Preservation Division, National Park Service, United States Department of the Interior. Denver, Colorado, [1979].
Demos, John. *A Little Commonwealth: Family Life* in *Plymouth Colony.* New York: Oxford Univ. Press, 1970.
Deyo, Simeon L., ed. *History of Barnstable County, Massachusetts ....* New York: H. W. Blake & Co., 1890.
Doane, Alfred Adler. *The Doane Family.* 2 vols. 2nd ed. Boston: A. A. Doane, 1902.
Ekholm, Erik, and James Deetz. "Wellfleet Tavern." *Natural History.* 80 (Aug.-Sept., 1971), 49-56.
Frankell, Moses M. *Law of Seashore, Waters, and Watercourses. Maine and Massachusetts.* Wakefield, Mass., 1969.
Freeman, Frederick. *The History of Cape* Cod. *Annals of the Thirteen Towns of Barnstable County.* 2 vols. 2nd ed. Boston: W.H. Piper &Co., 1869
Hersey, William D. "Cape Cod: 17th and 18th Century Roads, with Particular Attention to the King's Highway. July 5, 1962." National Park Service, 1962. Unpublished typescript.
Kittredge, Henry C. *Cape Cod: Its People and Their History.* Boston: Houghton Mifflin & Co., 1930.
Langdon, George D., Jr. *Pilgrim Colony:* A *History of New Plymouth, 1620-1691.* New Haven: Yale Univ. Press, 1966.
Lowe, Alice A. *Nauset on Cape Cod:* A *History of Eastham.* Falmouth: Kendall Printing Co., 1968.
McManamon, Francis P. "The Cape Cod National Seashore Archaeological Survey. A Summary of 1979-1980 Results." *Man in the Northeast.* 22 (1981), 101-129.
———. "Prehistoric Land Use on Outer Cape Cod." *Journal of Field Archaeology.* 9 (1982), 1-20.

———. "Probability Sampling and Archaeological Survey in the Northeast: An Estimation Approach." *Foundations of Northeast Archaeology.* New York: Academic Press, Pp. 195-227.

———. et al. *Chapters in the Archaeology of Cape* Cod. Division of Cultural Resources, North Atlantic Regional Office, National Park Service, United States Department of the Interior. Boston, 1984-1986.

Vol. I. "Results of the Cape Cod National Seashore Archaeological Survey 1979-1981." Volumes 1 and 2. Cultural Resources Management Study No. 8. 1984.

Vol. II. 'The 1983 Excavations at 19BN281." Cultural Resources Management Study No. 12. 1985.

Vol. Ill. "The Historic Period and Historic Period Archaeology." Cultural Resources Management Study No. 13. 1985.

Vol. V. "The Indian Neck Ossuary." Cultural Resources Management Study No. 17. 1986.

Miller, Perry. *The New England Mind:* From *Colony to Province.* Boston, 1961.

———. *The New England Mind: The Seventeenth Century.* Boston, 1961.

Morison, Samuel Eliot. *Samuel de Champlain: Father of New France.* Boston, 1972.

———. *The Story of the "Old Colony" of New Plymouth (1620-1692).* New York: Knopf, [1956].

Nye, Everett I. *History of Wellfleet from Early Days to Present* Time. Hyannis: F. B. & F. P. Goss, 1920.

Paine, Gustavus Treat. "Ungodly Carriages on Cape Cod." *New* England *Quarterly.* 25 (1952), 181-98.

Paine, Josiah Treat. *Eastham and Orleans Historical Papers.* Yarmouthport, 1914.

Pratt, Enoch. *A Comprehensive History, Ecclesiastical and Civil, of Eastham, Wellfleet and Orleans, County of Barnstable, Mass. From 1644 to 1844.* Yarmouth: W. S. Fisher & Co., 1844.

Rich, Shebnah. *Truro – Cape* Cod *or Land Marks and Sea Marks.* 2nd ed. rev. and corr. Boston: D. Lathrop & Co., 1884.

Snow, Dean R. *The Archaeology of New England.* New York: Academic Press, 1980.

———. *Foundations of Northeast Archaeology.* New York: Academic Press, 1981.

Stetson, Judy. *Wellfleet: A Pictorial History.* Wellfleet Historical Society, 1963.

Strahler, Arthur N. A *Geologist's View of Cape* Cod. Garden City: Natural History Press, 1966.
Swift, Charles F. *Cape* Cod. *The Right* Arm *of Massachusetts. An Historical Narrative.* Yarmouth: Register Publishing Co., 1897.
Synenki, Alan T., and Sheila Charles. *Archaeological Collections Management of the Great Island Tavern Site, Cape* Cod *National Seashore, Massachusetts.* ACMP Series No. 3. Division of Cultural Resources, North Atlantic Regional Office, National Park Service, United States Department of the Interior. Boston, 1984.
Wellfleet. First Congregational Church. *1723-1973: Two Hundred and Fifty Years of Worship*. [Wellfleet, 1973.)
Zuckerman, Michael. *Peaceable* Kingdoms: *New England Towns* in *the Eighteenth Century.* New York: Knopf, 1970

Reader Notes

About the Author

Durand Echeverria (1913-2001) was born in Short Hills, NJ. He received his college degree from Princeton University. During World War II, he served in the South Pacific with the US Navy. After the war, he returned to Princeton for his master's degree and Ph.D. in French literature. Echeverria then joined the faculty of Brown University, and during his thirty-year career rose to the chair of both its French and Comparative Literature departments. He published several books and was the recipient of two Fulbright Fellowships, a National Humanities Foundation grant and a Guggenheim grant.

After his retirement in 1980, Echeverria became a year-round resident of Wellfleet and an ardent conservation activist. He co-wrote Wellfleet's first shellfish management plan and was a principal writer of its harbor management plan, as well as a force behind the creation of the Wellfleet Conservation Trust. Wellfleet is indeed fortunate that he dedicated his research and writing abilities to preserving local history, resulting in this book *A History of Billingsgate – Before Wellfleet was Wellfleet.*

Photo courtesy of Wellfleet Historical Society and Museum

Made in the USA
Middletown, DE
08 August 2020

13663378R00073